Meeting Your Match

For Dale, who is the very best thing on the internet.

THIS IS A CARLTON BOOK

Published in 2015 by Carlton Books Limited
20 Mortimer Street
London W1T 3JW

10 9 8 7 6 5 4 3 2 1

A CIP catalogue record for this book is available from the British Library.

ISBN 978 1 78097 536 8

Senior Executive Editor: Lisa Dyer
Managing Art Director: Lucy Coley
Design: Sunita Gahir, Anna Matos Melgaco and Barbara Zuñiga
Production Manager: Maria Petalidou

Printed in Dubai

Meeting Your Match

Navigating the Minefield of Online Dating

Daisy Buchanan

CARLTON
BOOKS

Contents

Introduction

Once upon a time, internet dating was the preserve of people who had most of their erotic encounters alone, in broom cupboards. If you had to draw an internet dater in a game of Pictionary, you'd probably etch something that looked a little like a cheeseburger, with legs. Finding love online had about as much appeal as looking on Death Row, in the bookies or at a fungal infections clinic. Now everything has changed forever.

One in five people meets their future spouse online. Of course we fall in love and have sex with people we find on the internet. It's where we trade imaginary hay bales and make jokes, where we work and plan nights out and look for houses and buy oxblood brushed suedette boots with a wonky wedge heel in a misguided attempt to cure our hangovers. We live online, and there are no axe-murdering strangers, just potential lovers we haven't yet met. Well, admittedly there are some axe-murdering strangers out there, but probably no more than you'd find in your average bar or local hardware store.

Internet dating is as thrilling and useful an invention as contraception or melted cheese. When you think about it, the old days were bad days. When you had to meet someone semi-sober in a badly lit club or sleep with all of your friends, then all of their friends, then everyone at work, or just couple up with whomever the wicked fairy betrothed you to at your christening, kindred spirits were harder to find. At best, all you had in common would be a tolerance for strong alcohol and the need for some kind of paid employment to fund that tolerance. Now you can find a tailor-made match. If your three greatest passions are lacrosse, artisanal cheeseburgers and cow tipping, you can find your soul mate within an hour, as long as you're prepared to key in a few different passwords and credit card numbers.

However, internet dating is *an* answer, not *the* answer. It's not a genre on its own. It's as infinite, fallible and flawed as people are. It can only put you in touch with people who already exist and want to date online too. It can't build you a perfect robot partner. And if it did, it would be no fun. It's more of an art than a science, the variables are unlimited, but sometimes it can create an astonishing amount of chemistry.

This book can't tell you how to meet "The One" online and be happy forever. Nothing and no one can guarantee you a life of spouses and pies and adorable children and dogs. But we can make sure you have the very best chance of meeting a life partner and have a brilliant time while you're looking. You will need an open mind, an open heart and a thick skin. It will be fun, sexy, joyful, occasionally painful and, more often than not, downright hilarious. If you're serious about meeting someone, don't take anything too seriously.

Anyone can be successful at internet dating as long as they know the difference between confidence and arrogance, and have a sense of humour. You will need to beware of the weirdos, but that's easily done once you have learned to spot the signs early on from their profile and messages. And on the subject of profiles, we can tell you how to make yours sparkling, sexy and compelling.

Picking the right place for your profile is as important as getting the profile right. Every dating site out there has a different feel and personality. We can tell you what sort of people you can expect to find on each one – and, importantly, whether they're going to be your sort of people. Once you've found the sites that work for you and have your profile up and running, you'll be bombarded with messages. It might seem overwhelming, but we can help you discover, with a bit of detective work, which suitors are for real and which ones are not all they seem.

Constancy is not rewarded in the online dating world, so there will be advice on how to make the most of multiples – juggling sites and date nights, and laughing it off when you get your date's name wrong. After all, your prospective partners are at it too – which means that as well as learning to let people down gently along the way, you might need some advice on how to stay confident in the face of occasional romance adversity. But chin up! It happens to the best of us.

Safety is paramount, and although the internet is a much cosier, more inclusive world than it once was, it's worth being wary. As well as taking care to stay safe physically, it's good to know how to cover your tracks and stay secure online, from not becoming Facebook friends with a date before meeting them to being careful about check-ins and location information.

We also show you how to find fabulous matches in unlikely corners of the internet. Facebook is a place to meet potential paramours too. You can also find dates on Twitter, Instagram, even LinkedIn. Just because they're not dating sites, it doesn't mean you can't use them as a site for dating.

Ultimately, online dating is exactly the same as regular dating, but bigger, potentially better and with much more scope for fun. You don't have to commit to everyone you meet, but you do have to commit to enjoying it, hopefully and fearlessly. If you focus on the process, rather than on an end goal, you'll get much more out of it. You're going to meet people you would never have encountered before, make new, non-romantic friends and feel your confidence soar. Everyone should give it a go, at least once. You might meet the love of your life. You might meet the brother or neighbour of the love of your life. You might get taken out on a bad internet date and meet the love of your life in a chip shop immediately afterwards. But you've got nothing to lose – and good times to gain. We'd wish you luck but you won't need it, as long as you stay positive and keep having fun.

Have Courage!

Once upon a time you'd
end up marrying your
next-door neighbour out
of sheer geographical
necessity…

CHAPTER 1

· · · · · · · · · · · · · ·

Finding Your Match

· · · · · · · · · · · · · ·

Picking the Perfect Site

The best bit about internet dating is that no hobby, need or niche is too specific to stop you meeting millions of like-minded people. You can be massively into marmosets, Malbec or medieval battle re-enactments, and there's not just a section on a site for you – there is a dedicated site itself. However, although some companies, such as **Uniform Dating**, **Divorced Dating** and **Christian Dating**, really spell out exactly who should sign up and whom they can expect to find, other sites are more subtly specific. You'll find a certain sort of person on **Match.com**, and it isn't necessarily a pyromaniac. Similarly, the name **Guardian Soulmates** might sound like a self-published erotic fantasy novel but its members are more likely to be found up to their elbows in home-made hummus than silver latex.

Increasingly, desktop sites are losing ground to the new wave of dating apps. Many of these are location-based, so we've come full circle. Once upon a time, you'd end up marrying your next-door neighbour out of sheer geographical necessity, and now the internet allows you to sift through every potential match in the local area, probably leading you straight back into the arms of your neighbour. Still, now you can make a judgement call and work out whether or not you think they're hot before you pop round for a cup of sugar.

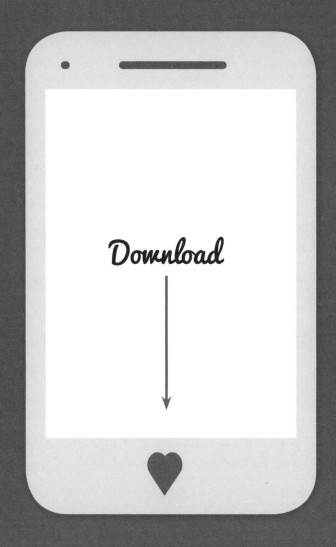

The great thing about apps is that once you've paid for a cripplingly expensive smartphone that comes with a five-year plan, they're usually free. You can dip a toe in the dating pool, and you're investing nothing but your dignity.

And anything that doesn't require a financial outlay is going to attract a huge amount of possible matches.

You have many more people potentially to play with. If you've been away from the dating scene for a long time – for example, for so long that when you first heard about sexting, you thought it was something to do with the academic work of Henry Miller – a free app is a good dating warm-up. It gives you a chance to assimilate a large amount of information in a very short time. Like a law conversion course, but with less Latin and more condoms.

Dating with Mates

If you can't contemplate finding a partner without the help of your pals, you will want to check out **www.mysinglefriend.com**.This is the perfect starting site for a reluctant internet dater, provided they can scare up a mate to write them a glowing reference. It's stuffed to the rafters with graduates in their twenties and thirties, who like pack activities. If you've ever been on an ironic group holiday to Pontins or gone paintballing with pals voluntarily, this is for you.

If you try it and love it, you might also enjoy **Grouper**. This site describes itself as a "social club", setting up meetings between groups of friends: you round up three same-sex single pals and they match you with a trio of the opposite sex. The idea isn't to re-create the hellish "boys v. girls" dynamic of a school disco but to allow users safety in numbers, while daring them to pull some fairly dangerous-sounding stunts. At the time of writing, their website urges users to dance on tables and "play vodka roulette", activities that one assumes are not covered by any insurance policy.

In the best-case scenario, one finds fun and romance, meeting a great date and fabulous new friends. There are numerous ways, though, in which it could go wrong. For example, everyone might fancy the same person, or you like one of them but think their friends are terrible, or there's no interaction between boys and girls, or someone gets confused and brings their dad. But you'll probably end up with something for your bank of funny stories, as well as discovering just how co-dependent you really are.

Queerly Beloved

If you're seeking a same-sex match, all the big sites should be able to hook you up with a potential partner (and if they can't offer anything to non-heteros, frankly they're too backward to actually be operating on the internet at all). However, some women understandably prefer dedicated gay dating spaces. **http://dattch.com/** works as a desktop site and an app, and the profiles are verified, so you know that everyone you speak to is actually female. **http://gaydargirls.com/** aggregates profiles from across the web, as well as providing a community space for swapping war stories and, hopefully, happy tales too. Brenda – **http://www.benderapp.com/brenda.html** – is relatively new to the scene and offers users video messaging, which can lead to whole new levels of personal paranoia, but if you're a Vine ace it might be the perfect way to meet the woman of your dreams.

Meet the Press

All British internet daters of a certain age are familiar – perhaps too familiar – with **https://soulmates.theguardian.com**. Although the site might have become a liberal punchline, the truth is that there's a lot to be said for ensuring your quarry is broadly on the same political page, otherwise you run the risk of having them ruin your third, brilliant date with the words, "Yes, of course I believe in executing the poor for stealing hares," forcing you to splutter so hard you lose a mouthful of a perfectly good organic elderflower martini.

The *Guardian* is especially great for knitters, veg growers, box-set obsessives and anyone who's ever crashed their laptop because they had too many **change.org** tabs open.

The *Guardian* might be the best-known version but plenty of other publications offer dedicated matchmaking services for their readers. Go with your gut, and read the comments sections before you make the call. Certain broadsheets will put you in touch with "high net worth" individuals, who might sweep you away on their private jet only to launch into a three-hour monologue about how much they hate the Euro while you're up in the air. If a publication makes a feature of nubile young women and their boobs, there is a chance that someone you meet via their dating site will want to see yours before you're prepared to show them.

Thank Heavens for the Internet

Choosing your match on religious grounds might seem a bit nineteenth-century, but if you're serious about practising your faith, it makes a lot of sense. Historically, churches haven't just existed as places to pray. They're communities that allow like-minded people to come together, support each other, and build friendships and relationships. In fact, you could argue that the Church is the original internet, only I don't think any translation of the Bible features the expression "pwned".

Even if you don't attend services regularly, but you come from a religious family and it's important to them that you find someone of the same faith, a site like **christianmingle. com** or **jdate.com** might be worth investigating. Otherwise, the differences that don't seem like a big deal over a flirty dinner might become deal-breakers five years later, when Great Aunt Rosa tells you she's launched a petition banning you from having a church wedding.

Rich Date, Poor Date

Seemingly on opposite ends of the spectrum but both aimed at the very broke, there are the free sites for people with no money, like **OKCupid** and **Plenty Of Fish**, and the sites for those who are hoping to make some money, like **Seeking Arrangement** and **Sugardaddie.com**. Now, dating should be a democratic affair, and available to everyone, whether they start the day with a breakfast swim in their coin vault à la Scrooge McDuck, or are so cash-strapped that they count partially stamped coffee shop cards among their bankable assets. But you do get what you pay for. To make an analogy that horribly objectifies your prospective matches, a free site can be a little like the clearance bucket in an outlet store: you might find something that suits you perfectly but you'll need patience, tenacity and a clear day in your diary.

Then there are sites where the transactional element goes beyond a conversation about who is going to buy the first round. They're operating within the bounds of the law and they are technically for dating. But if you're looking at them and hoping you'll end up falling for the billionaire of your dreams, it's time to turn down the *Pretty Woman* soundtrack and have a good think about what you might be letting yourself in for.

True or false?

Some dating sites are exceptionally niche. Can you work out which of the following might actually help you find your match, and which are completely made up?

1 darwindating.com Online dating for beautiful people only!

2 womenbehindbars.com A matchmaking service for women in prison.

3 theuglybugball.com Dating for the aesthetically average.

4 fivefingerfling.com Find love with fellow shoplifters.

5 realitylove.org Meet the former reality show star of your dreams.

6 candobetter.com For people who are already part of a couple but believe themselves to be significantly hotter than their spouse or partner.

7 clownpassions.com For clowns and the men and women who love them.

8 stairfree.co.uk A site especially for people who live in bungalows for medical reasons.

9 Cupidtino A dating app dedicated to fans of Apple products.

10 glutenfreesingles.com A site for people with compatible allergies.

11 **gothicmatch.com** A way to connect with singles from the gothic and emo communities.

12 **kardashiandating.com** Where fans of America's most famous sisters can connect.

13 **datingdip.com** Meet other honeys who love hummus as much as you do.

14 **seacaptaindate.com** Find your first mate.

15 **whatsyourprice.com** Auction yourself off to the highest bidder! It's sexy and not weird!

16 **farmersonly.com** Get agricultural or get out.

17 **pastlovespastlives.org** Meet your dead ghost love from olden days.

18 **footfetishpartner.com** For people who really, really, really like shoes.

19 **petloverdating.co.uk** If you struggle to choose between your partner or your puppy, this is for you.

20 **www.theatlasphere.com/about** For daters who are keen to meet other fans of Ayn Rand.

Answers

The dating sites in 4, 5, 8, 12, 13 and 17 are made up. The rest exist. This is all the proof you need that it doesn't matter how niche or novel your interests are. There isn't just one person out there for you; there are enough to power a whole separate internet server. In fact, the only people you might struggle to meet are the ones with severe technophobia. And chances are that **onlinedatingforpeoplewhorunscreamingfromtheinternet.com** will be up and running within a year or two. As for the rest, if there isn't a dedicated Kardashian dating site soon, those ladies are not as committed to capitalism as I previously believed.

Decoding Profiles

How can you tell anything about a person if you're not seeing them face to face? Can't they just lie in their profile? Indeed, they can and they do. Catfish (see pages 77–8) have a lot to answer for, but it's astonishingly easy to work out the truth if you know which clues to look for. Study profiles the right way and you can save yourself heaps of time that you might otherwise waste trapped in a messaging web or in a bar, drinking warm sauvignon with a person who collects belt buckles in the shape of swearwords. Here's the lowdown on the lie list – and the real meaning behind the words you're hearing.

"I work out a lot"

This is a dirty great inefficient euphemism for, "I can lure you to a meeting by pretending that I am toned and buff." Genuine gym aficionados will have a whole paragraph devoted to their fanatical belief in the power of free weights over cardio. You can call the bluff of imposters by asking for the name of their favourite brand of protein shake, but be warned – this might be interpreted as some sort of sexual come-on. This line is also adopted by men claiming to be wheat-intolerant as part of a fiendish plan to make their diet 100 per cent bacon. Ask if they're up for meeting over a frosty beer and see how they respond.

"My family is really important to me"

Well, that's good, in that it implies you, erm, haven't murdered any of them. Even the Kray twins loved their mum, after all. Again, this doesn't really need expressing, assuming they do the usual run of festive occasions, holidays and weekly phone calls. When a man feels the need to mention his family, read it as, "I have lunch at my nan's every Sunday and she gives me £20 out of her pension and the leftover roast potatoes." Or, "I already have a secret family, and I'm looking forward to starting a second one when I commit bigamy with you!"

"My job allows me plenty of opportunities to be creative"

 Nothing says "Please, please, please find me sexy!" quite like "I'm a creative!" No one will ever sell themselves as "a pragmatist with a flair for admin". The amount of time someone spends banging on about how creative they are at work is directly proportional to the amount of time they spend unnecessarily changing the font colour on Word documents, before their boss changes it back. These people will invariably send you unfunny chain emails written in rainbow Comic Sans. Anyone they deem less kooky and free-spirited than themselves will be nicknamed "Health and Safety". During dinner, they will wreck romantic moments by telling "Dad" jokes to the waitress. They will eventually ask to borrow five thousand pounds in order to entertain their true calling and take a degree course in Ceramics.

"I love animals"

What, in a casserole? When a dancing bear meme attracts more internet hits than a GIF of Kim Kardashian's undulating cleavage, and puppies are a more sought-after accessory than the latest iPad, surely it's only worth mentioning the way you feel about animals if you are allergic to them? This statement is dating-ese for, "If I associate myself with general cuddliness, you'll never guess that I also collect used underwear and I'm banned from the local department store changing rooms."

"I've never done this before"

The same people who spend their school days persuading anyone who will listen that they are not virgins are weirdly keen to promote their internet dating virginity. The lie means, "I have met people in real life, too. I was not born crouching over a hot screen trying to cross the line between flirting and mild sexual harassment." But anyone so keen to dismiss the tool they are using has the moral integrity of an abattoir owner dismissing concerns about cruelty because they're vegetarian.

"I like the finer things in life"

First of all, who doesn't?! Maybe Mother Teresa said, "No fine things for me, thanks; you keep the cookies and 500-thread-count sheets while I carry on looking after the orphans," but most of us are pretty fond of fancy things. This line is usually written by a guy who is hoping to imply that your life together will involve speedboats, premieres, caviar and hotels where the breakfast buffet will include tiny glass pots of high-end marmalade. However, anyone who says this sort of thing is usually a tedious idiot who wastes the energy of waiters sending back bottles of perfectly good wine because he thought he saw Kanye do it in a music video once. Also, no matter what kind of aftershave or cologne he wears, he will use far too much of it.

"Let me tell you all about the time I went travelling"

These words are usually spoken by men in their thirties who never quite recovered from their gap years. They speak of spiritual epiphanies, mind-bending experiences, sacred friendships and living in a more meditative way. But what they mean is that they went to Phuket with their rugby team, vomited for three days straight after a Full Moon party and have only just managed to get the beads out of their hair. These guys refuse to believe their experiences are identical to those of millions of tourists, even though they spent months in a country with millions of tourists. It's possibly because their observational powers are limited, and possibly because they managed to drink themselves blind using nothing but their dad's credit card.

"You'll have to meet my celebrity friends sometime"

 It's always worrying to think that the person whose profile you've clicked on has pegged you as a crazed autograph hunter who is so fame-obsessed that they regularly scour eBay to see if Britney Spears is selling any old clothes. Otherwise, why would they claim to be cool by celebrity association? To be honest, in this day and age it's hard not to have your own TV show. There are more celebrities than ever, so if you know any, it's not that big a deal. This person is pretending to have Madonna on speed dial, when they really mean that they once bought a car from the same dealership as a local radio presenter and now they wave to each other whenever they're both stuck in traffic.

"I like to unwind with a glass of wine and a DVD"

 It's amazing that this legendary cliché is still used by prospective daters, but it pops up all over the place. It can be translated as, "I'm lazy, really lazy, and I spend all my time at work and feel like a shellshock victim when I emerge from the office, blinking, at 10 p.m. I want you to think I'm quite cultured, but the wine is really Vimto with vodka in it. I don't own any DVDs either, just *Family Guy* GIFs I found on the internet. I definitely have a sofa, though. It's also my bed."

"My ex was crazy"

 Before you even know not to chew with your mouth closed when you go out for dinner, you know not to criticize or go on about your old partner. Anyone who makes allusions to the mental health of someone they used to sleep with, while speaking to a stranger, might just turn out to have been the crazy one all along. It's a short leap from, "My ex was crazy" to "You're behaving just like my ex" to… well, have you seen the film *Gaslight*?

Your photo should
say as much about
your personality
as it does about
your face.

CHAPTER 2

· · · · · · · · · · · · · ·

Planning Your Profile

· · · · · · · · · · · · · ·

Perfecting Your Profile

How do you, you fascinating figure, you thrilling and alluring beauty, you intellectual giant, darling of the pubs, legend of the people – how do you distil the intricacies and subtleties of your magnificent personality into one plausible-sounding paragraph? How can you show that you're a competent companion at work, rest and play, without mentioning your winter break in Val d'Isère or using the words "curled up", "cosy", "sofa", "DVD" or "glass of wine"? (Anyway, surely we're at the point socially where the mere mention of a DVD dates you more aggressively than an anecdote about that time you lost your ration book under the wheels of someone's penny farthing at the coronation of George V.)

Creating a dating profile is daunting. There is no way you can distil every exciting facet of your character in the space available. Writing about yourself is hard, but the process of editing yourself is so scary that brave men and women have given up and resigned themselves to a life of loneliness and fried-egg sandwiches because they can't quite bear to delete a very long, boring sentence that describes, in some detail, how they won a gymkhana in 1996. But take heart! It can be done – and done well.

When writing a profile, it's tempting to offer up the romantic equivalent of a gourmet burger. You want your words to have the weight and substance of high-quality beef, the crispness of grilled bacon, the erotic yield of three different kinds of melted cheese. But it doesn't matter how deliciously burger-y your profile is. It's going to be too filling. At this stage, the people you're looking to attract are only ready for a light snack or canapé. To mix metaphors further, you're creating a feast for the senses! The scent and sizzle of your words must entice a pool of romantic admirers to start clamouring at the door of your romantic kitchen! Your milkshake must bring all the boys to the yard.

And, at this stage, you *do* want to bring all the boys to the yard. There will be plenty of time to be fussy when the frenetic messaging starts. For now, you're not looking to frighten anyone off. By all means be detailed and discuss the most recent movie you watched and loved, or the last great meal you ate. But it's too early to talk about your daily breakfast pickled egg, your pathological, murderous hatred of border collies or that weird dream you keep having where Oprah Winfrey is your dad. Imagine you're introducing yourself to your best friend's colleagues at a party. Sound interesting, sound interested, and don't tell any long and rambling anecdotes about Jägerbombs, acid reflux and waking up in car parks. Let's get started!

"
Imagine you're introducing yourself to your best friend's colleagues at a party.

Get Confident, Stupid!

Before you get working on your profile, it's important to ensure you're in the right frame of mind. This might take an hour, a couple of days or a solid month. But it will be time well spent, I promise.

Being single affects our confidence in different ways. It can go up or down, depending on how your last relationship ended, the amount of time that has elapsed since, and your attitude to casual sex and socializing, and also on your relationships with friends, your work and your living arrangements. If you're thinking about online dating, chances are you're confident and curious enough to get a lot out of it. But it's well worth giving yourself a full mental health check before passing on your bank details.

Be honest. Would you date yourself? This doesn't mean that you have to dress up and book a dinner for one at the Hotel du Posh, toasting yourself with house champagne while reading a book called *How I Learned to Stop Worrying About My Excessive Underarm Sweat and Love LOVELY ME*. But you do need to be absolutely secure in the knowledge that you are an attractive and interesting romantic proposition. You don't necessarily have to change anything about yourself, but you might need to fine-tune your attitude.

First, think about your motives. Are you hoping initially to find someone fun and fanciable, who, if nothing else, will increase your pool of people to go for a drink with? Or are you convinced that you're not enough on your own, and that you'll only feel worthy of respect when you've found someone who will be there to celebrate birthdays, Christmases and Eurovision Song Contests? If it's the latter, you need a rapid infusion of self-love, pronto! Quickly, reach for the self-esteem defibrillators!

to my

Even Candace Bushnell, the patron saint of dating, said, "Better alone than badly accompanied." You can't look for love if you're feeling anything less than lovable. Any relationship that begins when you're in a bad emotional place is doomed from the start. Admittedly, the internet is full of people who are looking to date in order to shore up shaky self-esteem, but you're not going to be one of them, and if you do your homework early on, you'll be able to spot them before they digitally wink at you and save yourself a ton of future heartbreak.

Set aside 10 minutes and make a list of everything you like about yourself. It can be as broad, specific or downright daft as you like. No one else needs to see it. Be as generous as you would to your very best friend. "Knows perfect butter-to-Marmite ratio for toast", "Excellent at dancing alone in underwear", "Knows all the words to the rap in Justin Bieber's 'Baby'" would be fine things to put on such a list.

Then get ready to make another list, because dating is supposed to be difficult and you owe it to yourself to prep for it at least as hard as you did for your GCSE Maths retake. List every single thing that makes you happy. You can be soppy ("Holidays!" "Sunsets!") or silly ("Abba on the radio!", "Finding a 10-pack of jam donuts in Reduced To Clear!", "Seeing a traffic warden trip and fall off the pavement!"). Not only will these two lists eventually form a blueprint for your profile planning, they will remind you of all the things that make you sparky and special. Before you write your profile, spend at least a day trying to do as many things from the second list as possible. Don't try to make any traffic wardens trip over, but do pursue the stuff that makes you happy, and do your best to think about how good you feel as you're doing it.

The final part of the preparation process is this: CHILL THE FUCK OUT. The more relaxed you are in the run-up to getting started, the less likely you are to scare anyone off because you stink of desperation, and the less likely the experimental selfies you've been taking for your profile picture will resemble mug shots of a Gold Rush career criminal called Ol' Crazy Eyes. Guided meditation apps are great for helping you to clear your mind and work through any sense of anxiety you might have about dating. ("Headspace" is great, and there are plenty of freebies out there too.)

Essentially, you're training for a big game. Plenty of water, not too much booze. A little light exercise. Baths. Valerian tea. Delicious, nourishing food. Scented candles. Sleep. You need someone who's gonna treat you right, so treat yourself right first. Mariah Carey said that, probably.

And So to Work!

Now, as a reward for all your patience and perseverance, you may start writing your profile! Well, you've already made a start with your lists. It's good to remember everyone reading is in the same boat as you. It's a pretty big boat, more of a P&O ferry, but let's assume they're all, if nothing else, single and hopeful. For this reason, don't start, as so many profiles do, with the words, "So, online dating, eh? That's a bit weird! I don't really know what to write!" The reason the written word persists in this multimedia age is because people are still expected to maintain some sort of editing system so the rest of the world is not exposed to their unfiltered brain innards.

Remember that readers will probably know (or have guessed) certain things about you, depending on where you have placed your profile. If you've logged on to **fellwalkersfindlove.com**, you don't need to waste words stressing that fell walking is a massive part of your life.

Be positive. You can bond over the stuff you hate on your third date, when you get caught in the rain and end up in a bad Italian restaurant eating burnt spag bol. Under no circumstances must you get your profile mixed up with *Room 101*. If you focus on your anchovy allergy or your fear of finger painting, which developed after a very specific childhood trauma, you will attract oddballs, pessimists and people who are determined to introduce you to alternative artistic mediums and fish. Go back to your list and write about what you *actually like*. If you keep thinking of things you hate, go away and write an alternative list to get the grump out of your system.

This is not the place to start weeding out possible respondents – there will be plenty of opportunities to be choosy. Your profile should read like a friendly greeting to a big, virtual room, not a "KEEP OUT" notice that has been glued to a treehouse in order to deter small siblings. "Don't even bother to get in touch with me if you don't love cats (the animal)/*Cats* (the musical)/the earlier essays of Nietzsche" will pretty much guarantee that no one at all will bother.

However, don't be too positive. Don't feel that you need to write "I love sports!" or "I'm addicted to the gym!" if you perform all physical activities under a veil of cloudy tears and you just want to reassure possible love interests that you're no stranger to salad. Be specific. We all like going to the movies, but do you go to watch Armenian films about genocide that have no subtitles and last 17 hours, or do you prefer films with so many exploding robots that the heroine faints right out of her bikini? Don't say anything about "world cinema" for the sake of sounding intellectual – you might find yourself having to explain to a date that, technically, *Transformers 3* is a foreign film to you because you don't live in the States.

Describing your perfect date is a sweet way in. Think about how you'd want to entertain someone you were really into, if they were similar to you. If you'd genuinely want to go to a theme park or a zoo, that's fine, but if you're at your happiest over dinner and drinks, describe the cocktails you'd order and the dishes you'd pick. Obviously, don't finish with, "…and then we'd go back to mine for a good, hard shag."

Picking a Picture

Writing about yourself is a breeze compared with finding a photo of yourself that you actually like. According to research from eHarmony, profiles with photos are nine times more likely to get a response, so, unfortunately, this is a stage you can't afford to skip. You could try putting a statement in the box that reads,

> **"I find our obsession with outward appearance shallow, narcissistic and detrimental to the very fabric of society and demand that you give my profile fair and generous consideration based on nothing but the positive aspects of my personality."**

However, sensible fellow daters will read that as,

> **"I have cripplingly low self-esteem, which I unsuccessfully attempt to disguise by behaving like a complete tosser and using too many syllables. I'd love to go on a date with anyone at all, but we'll have to go to that fancy place in London where it's pitch-black and you won't be able to work out whether or not you're eating fried hamster, let alone what my face looks like."**

You're best off sucking it up and saying "cheese."

At this point in time, there is absolutely no excuse not to use a recent photograph. In fact, you can take a profile picture while you cook dinner, wait for a bus or run a bath (although perhaps not when you're *in* the bath). However, as hundreds of thousands of handsome men with hundreds of thousands of topless bathroom-mirror selfies to their name will testify, location is all-important. Your photo should say as much about your personality as it does about your face.

Most sites will let you upload a few different photos, so it's best to work in a mix of selfies and pictures of happy times you've had in the past. The statute of limitations on old pictures is about one or two years, as long as you haven't changed dramatically in the intervening time period. If you have subsequently lost or gained a significant amount of weight or hair, don't use the photo. A good guide is clothing: if you can still wear the jeans you were wearing when the picture was taken, you're golden. If there's something interesting happening in the photograph, you're giving the other daters the perfect platform for a conversation. ("Interesting" means you're petting a dog, posing by a rare telephone box or holding a beach ball – not standing in front of a crime scene, or clearly in the middle of an intense family fight.)

It's fine to include pictures where you're in a group, as long as there are a few solo shots too, and the browser can pick you out of the crowd without getting to the point that they stop looking for you and start looking for a bespectacled cartoon man in a red-and-white stripy hat.

"If you want to get a strong response, throw in a couple of pictures that wouldn't look out of place in a holiday brochure. Who doesn't love the beach?!"

Be careful with filters. It's OK to do a little cropping, editing and spot removal, but it's all too easy to go overboard and upload a set of pictures that will make everyone think you spend all your leisure hours travelling the country and going into those special dress-up booths for fake, old-timey portraits. It sounds obvious but it's often overlooked: the sun is nature's filter, and it's still the best one we've got. It doesn't matter how buff you are, you'll look better smiling against a bright blue sky than being muscly and moody in a dimly lit environment. If you want to get a strong response, throw in a couple of pictures that wouldn't look out of place in a holiday brochure. Who doesn't love the beach?!

Again, it sounds obvious, but it's worth saying. Do not use photographs where you're with your ex-partner. It doesn't matter how hot you look. If you're desperate not to waste the picture, crop them out. Admittedly, you might be stuck with a weird-looking chunk of their arm, but that's much less strange than having to explain their presence to the face of a stranger – especially as, unless the relationship ended on terrific terms, there's a strong chance you'll end up darkly cursing said ex, on your own, at the end of a first and only date, as you weep into a pint of wine. There's nothing wrong with a picture of you and a close pal of either gender, as long as you're not licking each other's faces and grabbing each other's crotches for a funny joke. Potential dates will not laugh.

If you work hard on your profile, you'll probably end up getting more out of other people's profiles when you start browsing, as you'll realize how tricky they are to put together and how hard it is to simultaneously sound interesting, intelligent and fun. It isn't easy, but the more you put in, the more you get out – this tends to be true of everything, apart from socks in the dryer, where the logic is mysteriously reversed.

Good luck!

Profile No-Nos

Under no circumstances must you write or do any of these things, unless you actually want to be alone forever:

• •

✖ Write your profile when drunk.

✖ Post any pictures to your profile that were taken in Malia, Kavos or Faliraki.

✖ Include details of fungal infections, cured and uncured.

✖ Make jokes about cystitis.

✖ Add hand-drawn diagrams of recent invasive surgery.

✖ Make allusions to the suspected extreme political sympathies of pop stars.

✖ Describe the last meal you ate that had fewer than three ingredients.

✖ Outline any sexual fantasies you have about quiz show hosts.

✖ List your ability to buy alcohol on a maximum-strength, minimum-cost basis as a "key life skill".

✖ List the most racist members of your family, in order of age and offensiveness.

✖ Attempt to enlist fellow daters in a pyramid scheme.

✖ Ask if anyone can tell you whether the weird thing on your arm is dry skin or leprosy.

✖ Refer to your passion for quinoa.

✖ Say that you're not sure if you ever want kids because, to you, all newborn babies look like aliens.

✖ Get too caught up explaining, in detail, any hobbies that involve chains, knives and saws.

✖ Describe any extra-terrestrial encounters you believe you have had.

✖ Discuss the last encounter you had with the police.

✖ Reveal you've never been sure whether your nipples were "really normal".

✖ Admit to accidentally killing any childhood pets.

✖ Admit to purposefully killing any childhood pets.

✖ Confess that you have a favourite astrologer.

✖ Justify the frequency with which you turn up to work drunk.

✖ Deploy any words ending in "-izzle".

✖ Outline your pet conspiracy theories and theorists.

lovelove lovelove
lovelovelo velovelove
lovelovelov ovelovelove
ovelovelovelovelovelov
velovelovelovelovelo
elovelovelovelovel
lovelovelovelove
ovelovelovelov
elovelovel

Are You Ready to Write a Profile?

It's time! You're poised on the dating diving board, ready to fling yourself into the pool of potential paramores from a great height, hoping to find yourself surrounded by people who look great in bathing suits while avoiding the floating human verruca plasters and suspiciously warm patches that have recently been vacated by relieved-looking swimmers. Yes, we're going to stop overextending metaphors and get signed up!

But are you really, really, *really* ready? Have you taken all of the lessons in, or are you still planning to start your profile with a two-thousand-word takedown of your ex, and specifically how they ruined your credit rating with their addiction to organic guacamole? Are you currently searching for a profile picture by going through every image in a file marked "Skiing, 2005"? Perhaps you're working out a way to incorporate the word "antidisestablishmentarianism" into the "About Me" section, to scare off all but the most hardcore spelling nerds? MISSION ABORT! YOU STILL HAVE MORE HOMEWORK TO DO.

This quiz will indicate whether you're ready to get going, or whether you need to spend more time sitting on your sofa with a glass of wine, learning how not to talk about how much you like to sit on your sofa with a glass of wine. Don't take it too seriously, it's just a bit of lighthearted fun. However, all instances of suspected cheating will be investigated. Please fill in all answers with a black ballpoint pen. Anyone using non-black ink will be frogmarched back to their local bookstore and forced to purchase another copy.

1

Which of the following people shouldn't be pictured with you in your profile photo?

A. President Obama

B. Your ex-boyfriend

C. Santa

2

"I'm really active! We should do something sporty together sometime!" If you receive this message, what activity should you suggest?

A. A lovely bike ride through a sun-dappled forest.

B. Watching a sporting movie, such as *Dodgeball* or *Caddyshack*.

C. A set of 50k lift reps, followed by a romantic dinner of raw egg yolk.

3

Sex is...

A. Something you're up for when you meet someone special online.

B. The name of the Instagram filter you've used on your picture.

C. The first word of your profile.

4

Weirdly, a complete stranger runs up to you on the street and says, "Describe yourself to me!" Which answer is the closest to the one you'd give?

A. "I'm confident, cheerful, I work in sales and I like dogs!"

B. "Single, ready to mingle, but you know, hopefully married by next Christmas. Are you single?"

C. "Not great today, to be honest. My skin condition has really flared up again."

5

How was school?

A. The usual – awkward, bad haircuts, but I still have a few pals from the old days.

B. Great, in fact, nothing has changed! Every night in the pub is a reunion.

C. I saw my old Maths teacher in town the other day and I had to hide in a bush.

Mostly As: You're ready for love!

The old song goes that you're nobody until somebody loves you. But you're already somebody – sane, sensible, and one suspects, in possession of a functional bank account. Which means that you're charming and probably well-adjusted enough to do very well at the internet dating game. Remember that it's an adventure, and you're increasing the odds of finding love, but you're not going to encounter anything different from real life. Just more of it. You might have all the common sense in the world, but that doesn't mean your internet dating experience is going to be freak-free.

Mostly Bs: You get an A for effort, but an F for Frightening

It's lovely that you're so keen, but you might want to dial it down a tad. No one's desperation should be detectable through a DSL line. You might not like being single, but it's not a disease. The danger of being so enthusiastic is that it suggests you don't feel like a whole person on your own. If you don't sound as if you like spending time by yourself, none of the single people on the internet will want to spend time with you either. Try to relax and enjoy your good points before you get started.

Mostly Cs: You've found your niche. And it's too niche.

You are gloriously comfortable with yourself. You're the only one in a buttoned-up world who could turn up to a date in a dressing gown, with the cord undone. Your self-knowledge is at a joyful peak. And your honesty means you're going to encounter people who will appreciate your eccentricity – but it will put quite a lot of people off. Ensuring your brain thinks of the words that are going in your profile *before* your fingers type them will mean that you end up with a few more matches. It's nice to have options.

The guy who will always
stand out in my mind is
the one who sent me
a picture of himself
shirtless and surrounded
by rubber ducks,
with no explanation.

CHAPTER 3

· ·

Learning From Others' Mistakes

· ·

Smart People Can Say Stupid Things

Sometimes the internet is a little bit like school: one person gets called out in front of the class and we learn through their humiliation and embarrassment. It's also like school because you're always worried someone is going to notice you're crap at sports and make fun of your haircut, but that's another matter. Anyway, sometimes you have to be cruel to be kind, and it's only by brutally mocking the errors of others that you can contribute to the general betterment of the online dating community.

Part of the reason we find the process of online dating so traumatic is because we're haunted by these bad examples. Setting up a profile that reflects you and your interests is easy, but some people manage to make it look very, very hard to come across as nice, normal, non-terrifying human beings. Some people are so scared about alienating any potential love interests that they sound bafflingly vague, like a boy-band member who's afraid to specify a particular favourite flavour of ice cream, lest he alienates any fans and potential sponsors. If you're tempted to write about your love of "music" or "the movies", you might want to think about this for a bit.

Then there are the people who are so determined to sound natural that they scorn the idea of editing their profile and fling the words down with such breathless impatience that one assumes they were setting up their account while being pursued by a bear. There are people who post photographs with exes, dirty laundry and guns, and those who sign off with the words, "Anyway, *ciao* for now!" There are those who don't know the difference between a dating profile and a party political broadcast, the ones who use a thousand words to paint a picture of the birthmark on their bottom, and the ones whose emotions transcend words and can only be expressed by punctuation that has been arranged pictorially.

There are plenty of bad profiles, but I believe the proportion of people with genuinely bad or bizarre intentions is actually very small.

The poorest examples are born from panic. You can see the stress and anxiety that their construction has caused. The internal monologues probably run along these lines: "Hobbies and interests? I can't think of any, other than watching TV with a beer! I can't put that. Um, what am I watching? A show about snakes? OK, I'll put 'snakes'." Weeks later, miles away, you're wondering why your profile has been "favourited" by a creep with a reptile fascination.

Sometimes smart people say the stupidest things, and while it's not kind to zero in on someone else's mistakes just to mock them, it can be incredibly comforting to know that very few profiles are perfect. Getting a sense of what to expect helps you manage your expectations, and it will make you feel much more confident about promoting yourself – laugh and learn.

Word Weirdness

Reading some of the stranger dating profiles is a great way to remind yourself of the power of the written word. Some phrases will sound great in your head, but completely crazy when read aloud. It's the difference between how good you think your voice is when you're singing Kate Bush songs in the shower, compared with how you'd actually sound were you to take to the stage at Carnegie Hall. Ultimately, your bio is a commercial and you don't want to write anything that would give the advertising standards people good grounds to fine you.

It's a bleak note to begin with, but you might notice that quite a few people frame their introduction with the words, "I'm quite *lonely*." Does that phrase make you want to donate to a social isolation charity, weep into a kitten and/or take a home-made cake to your nana? Almost certainly. Or does it make you think, "Hot diggity damn, that person sounds like a laugh riot, and foxy to boot!" Unless your proclivities are very specific, you'll almost certainly be turned off before the second syllable. It's evident that you might be a little bit lonely because you're looking for a stranger to share your life with, but there's no need to say it out loud. Be careful about using any words that make you sound like the beneficiary of a telethon.

Many more profiles are written by romantic hopefuls who are "great at massage" or who claim to be good with their hands. Innuendo is a big ol' innuend-NO. Anything even slightly sexual should only come up when you've made contact with someone, unless you're on a specialist adult site – and, in that instance, your sensual side is already evident because you're signed up for specific sexy dating.

"Banter" is a phrase beloved by the would-be dater. It's supposed to conjure up bell-like peals of laughter, the growing guffaws triggered by an inappropriate but hilarious joke told in a balmy pub garden on the first sunny day of the year. Instead, it looks, at best, a little lazy. It says, "I'm funny, but not so funny that I can think of something off the top of my head to make you laugh as you read my profile." It also says, "I laugh hysterically when I see pictures of things that look like boobs, and if we ever do have sex, I will refer to it as either 'doing it' or 'bonking'." Banter needs to be banished, and if you baulk at seeing it in other people's profiles, be very careful about using it in yours.

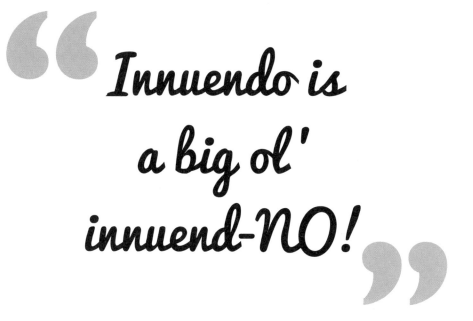

Innuendo is a big ol' innuend-NO!

We've also learned to be wary of people who say, "I'm looking for something special" or "I'm after something a little bit different." We all know what they're hoping to convey, right?! Love is unique! Romance is glorious, and they're seeking the special snowflake who will turn their lives upside down. They want you to know that if you fall for each other, every day will be magical and you'll never spend an evening lying on the sofa in silence, slack-jawed and up to your elbows in Doritos. The sentiment is lovely, but the execution is lazy. We all want "special" and "different", but you need to spell it out and show your workings. If you're tempted to use the "s" word, seeing it appear on every other profile you view will put you off it forever. Similarly, watch out for people who list three hobbies and add, "… and lots more!" In this instance, "lots" means "eating, sleeping and a little intimate scratching when I'm home alone."

You will be amazed by how many people mention their exes. Do not think this means it is now OK to mention your exes. Keep your head in the game, and don't be tempted to refer to your broken heart, even if everyone else is doing it – even if you encounter your own ex and discover they have set up a profile slating your taste in music, your tendency to snore and your inability to make decent pancakes. That said, some of the least appropriate matches will lead to some of the most enjoyable reads. Look out for highly entertaining descriptions of disputed coffee tables and goldfish custody battles.

" *If you're tempted to use the " s " word, seeing it appear on every other profile you view will put you off it forever.* "

" *Ultimately, the most important thing about the picture is that the subject should be smiling, and both eyes need to be open and focused on the same point.* **"**

Picture Imperfect

How hard is it to take a photograph? *Really hard*, if the internet examples are anything to go by. If someone seems great in all other respects, you probably shouldn't discount them straight off the bat just because their chosen avatar is a selfie in which they are standing next to an ironing board piled high with empty tuna cans. Maybe they were on their way out with the recycling and got distracted because they were so excited about taking their profile picture. Whatever the reason, such photos are to be avoided.

The setting is important. Parks, beaches, celebrations, most landmarks, occasions at which people have had a little alcohol – all good. Dirty houses, offices, occasions at which the guests have enjoyed themselves so intensely that their pupils resemble reddened golf balls, landmarks commemorating death or tragedy – these must be avoided. It shouldn't warrant discussion, but if it didn't, there wouldn't be a blog collating dating site profile pictures that were taken at the Holocaust Memorial in Berlin.

Ultimately, the most important thing about the picture is that the subject should be smiling, and both eyes need to be open and focused on the same point. A good way to check whether a photo passes muster is to see whether you could enter it in a caption competition. If the best phrase you can come up with is something like, "Cheerful woman stands next to hedge," the picture is insufficiently ridiculous, which means it's safe to click, and a fine example to follow for your own avatar. If you'd title the picture, "No shoes, no shirt, possibly bottle service," or "Check out the gun show – and the arms aren't bad either!", it's best avoided as an inspirational source as well as a romantic one.

When Messages Misfire

Sometimes you can make it past the profile round only to discover that your game falls apart as soon as you click that winking envelope icon. Why is it so hard to find the words to tell a stranger that you find them attractive and wonder if they'd care to join you for a drink, a dance or a trip to the zoo?

Again, the pressure to perform can lead a person to say, or type, the strangest things. If you receive a "DTF? ;)" message, it's not a sign that society is declining and we're heading for a *Mad Max*-style collapse, in which everyone gives up on communication entirely and spends their days chasing each other with chrome and leather dildos. It's a combination of fear and laziness that some people are better at managing than others...

The first five messages should contain nothing you wouldn't want to put in a work email that your boss could potentially read aloud to the office. Dirty jokes, abbreviations and pictures of swans and humans performing intimate acts of congress should not make the cut. Helen, a publisher in her early forties, reveals, "One guy would not stop sending me pictures of animals having sex. To be fair, I thought the first couple were quite funny, but once he'd worked through dog sex, deer sex and dolphin sex, I had to block him. Seriously, what is wrong with people?!"

Spelling is a controversial conundrum. In the red corner, we have the daters who can't abide a misplaced comma, much less a hopeful romantic who can't manage all the syllables in "evening" or "martini". And in the blue, those who think stressed-out spelling perfectionists are anal idiots who don't deserve to find love.

If you have genuine political objections to proper spelling, it might be better to make those apparent from the word go by coming up with some crazily creative arrangements of letters. However, it's always better to err on the side of the *Oxford English*, if you can force yourself. Lucy, a teacher in her thirties, admitted, "Perhaps it's because of my job, but I can't bear it when people don't at least make an effort with spelling. I've had messages where every other word was wrong, including books and bands I'd mentioned in my profile and spelt correctly! Occasionally I've got drunk and replied, highlighting and correcting all the errors, which I admit was very mean. At least I didn't write, 'See me' at the end."

Another thing to be wary of is chat-up lines. The joy of dating online is that you're not in a bar. Yet some people are determined to pass up all the modern conveniences at their fingertips and ruin their prospects the old-fashioned way. "Why would anyone begin a message with, 'Was your father a thief, because he must have stolen the stars from the sky to make your eyes?'" wails Natalya, a software analyst. "We're postmillennial. Yet some guys out there are still labouring under the misapprehension that this constitutes original content. What about 'Hey, baby, was your father a thief, because I saw him looking shifty with a car stereo under his arm and I've a good mind to report him to Neighbourhood Watch?' That would be a little more original."

Be Yourself, Everyone Else Is Already Taken

A weird experience shared by everyone who dips their toe into the lukewarm communal leisure centre pool of internet dating is that sometimes you'll attract disgusting, used, soggy Elastoplasts masquerading as Hollywood stars. Elena, an illustrator, admits, "I found this really hot guy when I was browsing profiles and showed his picture to my friend, who looked closely and said, 'Isn't that a very old picture of Daniel Day-Lewis, the actor?' If it was the real Daniel Day-Lewis, I don't think he would be masquerading as a software developer living in the Midlands. Also, if it was the real Daniel Day-Lewis, someone needs to tell him you can't use a photo from 10 years ago."

Here's a tip: if it's true, you can write something along the lines of, "My friends tell me I look a little like *Friends* actress Jennifer Aniston." You cannot use a picture of Jennifer Aniston, even though it would be easy to do so since you don't have to bother cropping out any man next to her because magazines have given us a decade's worth of pictures pointing out that she is "so alone". Also, be wary of people who appear to be frolicking in suspiciously symmetrical meadows, grinning at photogenic food or looking self-important in front of a pie chart, unless their bio states that they are employed as stock photography models.

Worse than the false photo is the stolen profile. Some unscrupulous users have been known to copy and paste the best bits from other people's profiles, playing a verbal game of Misfits and creating a mutant master dater, a flirty Frankenstein's monster with a head that doesn't match the legs. Stacey, a barrister, said that she spotted something was amiss when two guys both claimed their bands were playing at Glade Festival.

"At first I thought it was hilarious that I might have been matched with two musicians who were going to be in the same place, and my friends and I were plotting how I might spend a romantic weekend running between two different tents. But when I looked closer and realized the wording was the same in both profiles, and one guy had uploaded loads of pictures from gigs and the other looked less rock'n'roll than my dad, I realized I'd been duped. I've no idea why someone would do that, but it does happen."

Remember, imitation might be the most sincere form of flattery, but straight-up plagiarism isn't on.

Unclassifiable

Some human behaviour defies all logical explanation. Occasionally…
OK, frequently, you will encounter people online whose freaky and
unrealistic expectations cannot be categorized. We may not be able to
analyze the mistakes these daters make. All we can do is collate them and
marvel at them.

Cassie, 28:

**"One guy messaged me, saying
he was looking for a glamorous,
attractive partner to take to a
high-profile tennis event. His
second paragraph began, 'Of
course, before the event we
would need to meet regularly
for robust sex to convince
everyone else in attendance
that we are a couple.'"**

Joe, 38:

"I was regularly messaged by a woman who wrote everything as a limerick. The first one was cute. I ignored the rest, and they started to become abusive."

Annette, 42:

"The guy who will always stand out in my mind is the one who sent me a picture of himself shirtless and surrounded by rubber ducks, with no explanation."

Roshni, 24:

"The same man has found me on FOUR different dating sites and sent me the same message: 'RU into leather?'"

Kim, 46:

"I'm ashamed of how humiliating I found this, but a man that I was in no way attracted to messaged me to say, 'It's a shame about your nose. If it wasn't for that, I'd definitely date you.' I know those are the words of a person with all sorts of issues, but it made me cry."

David, 24:

"I liked the woman whose profile listed the London parks she was not prepared to visit on dates because they reminded her too much of her ex."

Steffie, 34:

"One guy's profile began with a reference to how he was a bit of a foodie – great! – and ended with a 500-word diatribe about how he liked to order a whole spicy chicken at his favourite chain restaurant and refuse to share it with anyone. Apparently, sometimes he sent the chicken back, which 'proved' he had 'very high standards'."

Mark, 38:

"A few matches have loads of pictures of their kids in their profile, which is awesome – I mean, don't hide the fact that you're a proud parent – but they don't upload any photos of themselves. I find that weird."

Jenny, 40:

"The one that still makes me laugh is the man whose profile was just a list of his measurements. Calf, upper thigh, waist, hips, even neck. I hope there's someone out there who just loves to see body measurements written down. If he's going to find her anywhere, it's going to be on the internet."

Aziz, 22:

"One guy didn't bother to introduce himself or say hello, but sent me 10 fairly specific trivia questions about wrestling champions. I had not mentioned wrestling in my profile, and neither had he."

Angelique, 39:

"When it comes to dating, I'm pretty open-minded about meeting older guys, but there was one whose first message contained the baffling line, 'Because I'm much older than you, I'll have to teach you how to wash my car.'"

No dashing stranger
is going to send the
digital version of the
coroneted billet-doux.

CHAPTER 4

• • • • • • • • • • • • •

Message
Madness

• • • • • • • • • • • • •

Instant Communication

Anyone who has been on the internet dating scene for more than 48 hours will know that the old-school love note is a thing of the past. No dashing stranger is going to send the digital version of the coroneted billet-doux – but you will quickly be confronted with new and bewildering acronyms, such as ASL and DTF.

We all communicate in different ways, and plenty of us speak or think with great fluency and fluidity but struggle to get it down on paper or in pixels. (Some of us really only come into our own when we're playing Pictionary, but that's a different story.) If you don't enjoy writing, it's easy to approach the messaging element of online dating in the same way that you might approach a dangerous, escaped bear: subtly, wary of the importance of self-preservation, and fearing that you might get eaten alive.

However, if you force yourself not to take any of it too seriously, the messaging comprises some of the most fun you'll ever have on the internet – excluding Candy Crush, obviously. If you spend too much time worrying about it, you'll make it feel like a gloomy, unending sex-and-love exam you haven't revised for. But refuse to overthink it, and you'll soon feel like the Mayor of Dating Town, which, realistically, is probably your nearest All Bar One.

Culturally, I suspect we all struggled when we took up texting. As teens, we thought that one day we'd grow out of staring at screens, fearing our words would be misinterpreted and that we'd be laughed out of town for using the wrong winking emoticon. In my day, the stakes were much higher, because you had to make your own emoticons out of punctuation marks. But as we've discovered more and more technology that enables us to talk to each other, we've become increasingly paranoid and frightened. There are more ways than ever to get it wrong. Everyone has a story about, "That time I hit 'Send' by accident and my world imploded over the course of a weekend." This means that, when it comes to messaging, we're spooked and running scared.

However, the good news is that, since we spend 90 per cent of our waking hours hunched over a keyboard of some description – actually, it's probably longer because, let's be honest, we all tweet on the toilet – we're better at online chat than ever. We're all constantly using and building our writing skills, learning how to incorporate wit, nuance and detail into our words, which makes us well placed to communicate with the dating world.

The first few messages you send might seem a little clunky and awkward. Think back to your first ever part-time job. How often were you forgiven for setting off fire alarms, dropping plates or standing open-mouthed as a local robber made off with the day's takings simply by saying, "Sorry, I'm new"? Well, it's the same deal here. If you start with the words, "I haven't done this before," you can melt the hearts and soften the minds of any more seasoned messenger. Just don't try to get away with it after your first couple of weeks.

"I Just Wanted to Say 'Hey'"

Most dating sites will offer a "sub-message" option, which allows you to wave at, "heart" or poke or prod anyone with a profile that you like the look of. Leave this whole area alone. As long as your subscription allows you to do so, it's always far better to send a short message than spend weeks locked in a stupid online battle of tag. You might as well find the person in real life and tap them on the shoulder repeatedly while saying, "Oi! Sex, then?"

Ditch any old-fashioned notions you have about gender – who should pursue and who should be pursued. You're not paying a monthly subscription to stand around looking bored at a weirdly retro digital cotillion. Fortune favours the brave, and if you're not going to be brave, you'll waste a fortune.

First-time messages often fail because they end up reading like a breathless, panicked voicemail – you know, the ones that go on for half an hour because you can't stop talking and can't help but give graphic details of your most recent gynaecological exam, without managing to explain who you are. Which is probably for the best. It sounds obvious, but it's amazing how difficult it can be to filter your train of thought and craft your message instead of vomiting the entire contents of your brain into your sent message folder. If you need proof, look in your inbox. You're going to get plenty of messages from people who seem completely crazy, but the truth is that they're just struggling to stay calm.

Most of the information you want to write is already in your profile. Make sure your message focuses on a detail you have seen in their profile. It's better to pick something cerebral. "I'd love to talk to you about your degree in Art History," is going to go down better than, "I really liked the look of your hot bod."

Don't suggest a meeting straight away but ask a detailed, engaging question that will make them want to respond. It doesn't have to be personal, but it's great to choose something general to which there might be a specific response.

" *Fortune favours the brave, and if you're not going to be brave, you'll waste a fortune.* "

Here is an example of a strong message:

Dear Sailor Jerry

Hello! Hope you're having a good day. Your profile caught my eye thanks to your interest in nautical history. I just watched a documentary about smugglers' boats, and it's something I'd love to know more about...

I have a question for you. Would you rather be attacked by 10 duck-sized horses or one horse-sized duck?

Yours wonderingly,

Ann Online-Dater

Here is an example of a weak message:

Dear Sailor Jerry

HELLO! I just saw your profile and I thought you reminded me of that guy who was in the advert for that thing where they glued shelves to the wall. Was it you? Actually, it might have been for cereal. Anyway, I'd really like to meet you. I'm 28, I have my own hair and teeth. (Ha-ha! Actually, I do wear hair extensions but it's real hair. In fact, I think the hair comes from the woman who runs the salon. I can probably introduce you if you like!!!) I see that you studied Chemistry at university. I did Geography, although it doesn't come up much in my job as an event planner, but I suppose I use it when I'm telling people where to have the events. I live on Oak Road with two housemates. I get on with one, and the other is in trouble because she finished off my brie without asking last week and has yet to replace it. And I think our boiler's broken, but the landlord claims it's because we have too many baths. ANYWAY, if you want to meet, I can do Tuesday, Thursday or Friday next week, but I'm at a wedding at the weekend (my ex will be there – eeek!). I'm quite into Turkish food at the moment but I'm off pizza because of my IBS.

Looking forward to hearing from you,

XXXXX

Balls in the Air

Messaging is a sport, and not every player is of equal ability. Some will outclass you immediately while you're still struggling to work out which way you should be holding the racquet. As your skills improve, you'll encounter people who knock your balls right out of court and into the garden of an angry neighbour. And some people will refuse to learn the rules and return your every serve with the words, "SEND NOODZ". When the process feels like a thrilling, addictive game, it's because you're generating a real spark with the person you're messaging, and they're worth pursuing. But if it doesn't feel like it's working out, don't worry. Two people can adore each other's profile pictures but struggle to find anything to say to each other beyond that. It's not that there's anything wrong with you, or them – you're just not right for each other.

Part of playing the message game involves knowing when to call time on it. You need to convert a message to a meeting fairly speedily, or you'll be lost in the online ether forever. Hopefully, it will be as easy as saying, "I think we should do this in the pub." Ideally, they will be savvy and switched-on enough to get in there first, but don't wait to be asked. The better the messaging goes, the more pressure there will be on that first meeting. Be wary. Great messaging can be addictive, but it's not what you came for. You want your real-life interactions to be the ones that benefit from your charm and energy, not your online ones. Don't let the messaging get to the stage where any human contact can only disappoint you.

Framing the Catfish

Most of the people you meet online will be honest and genuine. They might not immediately tell you about their relaxed sock-washing policy or teen shoplifting habit, or the enormous mole on their back, but, for the most part, they will be as they present themselves: single people looking to meet other single people and find a relationship.

However, pop culture has introduced us to the Catfish – the online lurker who forces us to fall in love with them and subsequently disappears, often after creating a made-up name, persona and a string of fake friends. Catfish are rarer than TV might suggest, but they do exist, and they love messaging.

The biggest clue that you're stuck with a Catfish is their unwillingness to meet in real life, and their string of improbable excuses. The trouble is, at that point you're in so deep that you desperately want to believe they can't come for a drink with you because they have to drive their sister across the country to see a jelly bean allergy specialist, or because they must accompany their dog to its debut in the Moscow State Circus. So, ideally, you should be on the lookout for Catfish signs throughout.

For starters, Catfish generally message first. Someone you contact is less likely to contrive a fake persona, because being a Catfish takes planning. It isn't a hard-and-fast rule, but it's worth bearing in mind.

Catfish are almost always too good to be true. If you get a message from someone exclaiming over the improbability of your perfectly matched profiles – what are the odds of finding another fourth-century gamelan fiend? – be suspicious. Their motives vary, and these are as likely to be psychological as criminal. Of course, if anyone you meet online wants your money, sever all contact straight away, no matter how strong their story.

Not all Catfish are looking to fleece you. There are a variety of reasons why you'd pose as someone else online, and they're all unhappy ones. Presenting yourself as the perfect person is easy on the internet, and it's also easy to find strangers who will fall in love with the facade you have created. We all want affection, attention and validation, and some people will go to any lengths to get it. Hopefully, they will find the help they need, but you shouldn't have to be part of their story.

In general, the messaging process can be overwhelming, frightening and frustrating. You'll know when you're getting it right, because it will start to feel fun. Try to trust yourself and your instincts. If something feels odd, shut it down, and if you feel especially relaxed about someone online, they will probably be a strong real-life match. You don't have to let your guard down completely for everyone, but know that most of the people messaging will have the same intentions as you.

> **❝ ...trust yourself and your instincts.
> If something feels odd,
> shut it down... ❞**

Message Understood

Everyone who's been around the digital dating block will have a few messaging horror stories. Rest assured that when it suddenly goes wrong, it's not you – at least, it's not *just* you. Here's a selection of the worst types of missive that you might find when you log on and look for love online.

The wannabe sub-editor

Good spelling is important. We all learned that at school, and our teachers would never, ever lie to us. Right? However, occasionally we might forget it's "I before E except after C", but you have to be a right C to point out a spelling mistake to a stranger before you've said hello. If a message is forcing you to take part in some unwanted student role-play, banish the sender to Dictionary Corner.

More boring than the Yellow Pages

There's nothing wrong with this person, but you can't read their message without hearing it in a dull, mechanical monotone. It isn't offensive, yet you're slightly offended that they think you might be interested in hearing anything so bland. You decide this is a person who couldn't have an independent thought if a lion chased them around its den for one. You automatically assume they drink the worst beer and like the worst movies, which they watch while wearing the blandest clothes. The message makes you angry with its ordinariness. You fester for days. You never reply.

The ghost message

You like pizza, they like pizza. You like long walks, they like long walks. You like trips to Italy, they like to disappear from the internet, never to be seen again. You'll never know whether they received a better offer, got back together with their ex or were threatened with a phone bill that meant they had to cut off their internet use completely. OK, so that last one is unlikely. But it could have happened.

The sexy scribble

You don't know them but they think it's appropriate to send you a detailed, modern-day retelling of the flower-festooning bits from *Lady Chatterley's Lover*. The stuff they're describing is so filthy that you're forced to ask your little sister to explain what some of it means, and you then spend the rest of your days in a haze of shame. You don't know why they thought you'd want to get down and dirty so quickly when they have seen one picture of you, in a plain white tee-shirt, pointing at a man on a plastic horse at Legoland. It's not that you don't like that sort of thing, but it's polite for a person to find out whether you like that sort of thing first instead of sending it to you speculatively. You suspect they've sent the same message to everyone, but it's no good pushing a leaflet for a chimney-sweeping service through everyone's door when you live in a bungalow. You block them, report them to the site administrators and threaten to tell their mums.

INK

The first date won't be the one. The tenth date probably won't be the one. But if you've been out of romantic circulation for a while, the early dates are a form of adult education.

CHAPTER 5

• • • • • • • • • • •

First Dates

• • • • • • • • • • • • • •

" Where Shall We Go?"

First, well done! You have put the time in online, and you've browsed through enough profiles to click with a person that you can imagine meeting in real life. Now everything is about to burst into full, glorious, 3-D Technicolor. It's very easy to stay logged on at home, where the waistbands are elasticated and the power of rejection is yours alone, but you're about to take a big risk – one that's worth taking – and it's important to be properly prepared.

Within reason, if you think you like someone, you will want to get to this point as fast as is humanly possible. The more you fall for them online, the more you have to lose and the easier it is to pass up their offer of a pasta dinner, deciding it's safer to spend the evening alone in your dressing gown, typing furiously and crying. Essentially, you're still at the start of your journey, so don't treat this bit as if it's the final stop.

On that note, it's vital to start by preparing for the worst as well as hoping for the best. The first date won't be the one. The tenth probably won't be the one. But if you've been out of romantic circulation for a while, the early dates are a form of adult education. It's like you're in *The Diving Bell and the Butterfly*, only you're working out how to eat in front of someone you don't know and listen to anecdotes while laughing in the right places, instead of failing to conceal your boredom and chewing a fork.

Within reason, it doesn't matter where you go, as long as you have a plan. There's nothing sexy about, "Um, I dunno, we could go to the pub?" There's nothing wrong with the pub, but let them know you have chosen it deliberately because of the fine beer garden and excellent chips. There's no need for cocktails at The Ritz, but you should pick somewhere that indicates you have given the matter some thought, not just chosen a place within walking distance from your house.

It's annoying, but the most helpful piece of advice is also conflicting: think about it, but don't overthink it. It's easy to control your dating universe from behind your computer but, to some extent, when you leave your screen, you have to loosen up. You won't be able to craft perfect jokes that require a quick Google to check obscure eighteenth-century property laws for the punchline. Trust that your brain will do the work of a thousand search engines. If you can't check yourself, you won't necessarily wreck yourself. Experienced dater Alison says, "Goodness, if I sat down and really thought about all the stuff that could go wrong, pre-date, I'd have a panic attack halfway through shaving my legs, and spend the rest of the night locked in my own airing cupboard. You just have to tell your brain, quite firmly, to shut up and let you get on with it."

> # There's nothing sexy about, 'Um, I dunno, we could go to the pub?'

Type and Timing

The way that most of us work and socialize dictates that most dates will be arranged for the evening, in a place that serves alcohol. But it's not your only option. Daytime dating is becoming increasingly popular, as it's a little less pressured and more flexible than being squeezed into a dark, dank, busy bar until closing time. Jessica, a stylist, says, "At first I thought that going on a daytime date was crazy, because for me, part of the fun lies in getting dressed up and drinking cocktails. But after a while I realized I was enjoying the date prep more than the actual dates. Going for coffee or lunch instead gave me a little valuable screening time, and allowed me to make sure I was only getting to the cocktail stage with people whose company I loved."

• •

John, an engineer, agrees:

"A couple of years ago I'd have said there was no way you could get me to have a conversation with a stranger unless I had a drink in my hand. But once you've got a couple of daytime dates under your belt, you realize it's not as scary as you'd expect it to be, and you've got a much more honest, open basis for a relationship. I've met some lovely girls who really weren't right for me, but we ended up going on three or four boozy dates before realizing the spark wasn't there. It sounds brutal, but starting off by going for a coffee or a sandwich saves a lot of time!"

The trouble with asking someone for a date is the politics of timing. We're all busier than ever, and having a packed diary is a bit of a status symbol. No one wants to ask out a brand-new date on a "premium" slot, like a Saturday night. You're expected to be so frantic and glamorous that every weekend for the next four months should be booked solid with nights out and trips and events with your core friendship group, even if the closest thing to a hot party in your diary involves a baked potato and a microwave. But when work, life, errands and various miscellaneous duties threaten to take over your week, sometimes Saturday is the only day that lends itself to meeting new people.

Penelope, an actuary, says, "I used to have this stupid policy of never being free for new dates on a Saturday night, but it just got ridiculous. I've found that Saturday or Sunday afternoon is perfect. If it's going well and you fancy drinks or dinner, you can segue into it really easily. And if you do need to bail, you can claim you have plans and no one is going to question that." Don't worry, the dinner date is alive and well – it's just not your first port of call on the, erm, romance ferry.

Obviously, the time-honoured pub date is a tradition that is in no danger of dying out, but it's worth making a plan before you get stuck into the pork scratchings. Should you fall in love and live happily ever after, there's nothing to stop you from spending all your future romantic meetings re-creating scenes from *Barfly*, other than your own good sense, government health recommendations and innkeepers who might refuse to serve you. However, if you're drinking on your very first date, there's nothing wrong with going soft on every other order. It's the difference between wearing beer goggles and being blinded by the misguided passion that's often generated by alcohol. If your date is a disaster, it's often tempting to drink until you fancy them, or at least until you can bear to listen to them without chewing on a beer mat out of sheer frustration. If your body is telling you to ingest more booze units before you burst into tears of boredom, listen to your mind instead and leave. That way you'll avoid a bad second date, and a hangover.

"If your date is a disaster, it's often tempting to drink until you fancy them, or at least until you can bear to listen to them...."

Mind Your Manners

The ideal first date venue is a place that is equidistant between your respective postcodes. However, because logic is a bastard, this means that you're likely to end up at a municipal tip, supermarket or car park, and not a delightful candlelit hostelry, tavern or, indeed, any setting conducive to a romantic occasion. Still, the rule is that it should be easy for both of you to make your separate ways home afterwards without anyone feeling obliged to order a ruinously expensive taxi or spend the night on a strange sofa.

It doesn't matter who suggests the date, but the person who asks should always include a venue suggestion. Never refer vaguely to "hanging out" and then wait for your possible match to pick a place or make a plan. It's rude. If you've got the guts to go online in the first place, you are more than capable of asking someone out properly. This isn't school.

If you have been asked on a date and you are interested in pursuing the person who made the suggestion, you should usually defer to their choice of location. However, there are two exceptions. First, if they have proposed that you go to a cafe or bar that is next door to their home, you should ask them outright what their intentions are. Second, if you have visited the named establishment previously and contracted food poisoning or the norovirus you'll need to name some alternatives.

Assuming the asking has gone without trauma or incident, it's time for some first-date prep! Numerous pieces of dubious research have claimed that the men and women of Britain spend anywhere between £50 and £600, and one to 14 hours getting ready

"
...your date probably won't notice the fact that you have spent upwards of three figures in a salon...
"

for this event. Do anything and everything that makes you comfortable, but be entirely honest with yourself about who is going to benefit from your efforts. If throwing time and money at the situation makes you feel more confident, so be it, but your date probably won't notice the fact that you have spent upwards of three figures in a salon, unless the effect makes you look like you've had a face transplant and you no longer resemble your profile picture.

The one bit of pre-date admin that might not hurt your cause is a quick crash course in current affairs. Katherine, a journalist, says, "My job has been brilliant for my dating prospects, just because I need to digest a lot of news in a short amount of time, and this means I'm never stuck for something to talk about. I don't necessarily go in on the heavy stuff. Although I'm really passionate about international politics, I appreciate that Syria isn't really the best topic for date chat. But there's always a daft survey out there, or a weird bit of news, or something adorable that got stuck up a tree... It's a great way to keep a conversation going, and ensure you both have something to talk about and can explore ideas and opinions, instead of the usual, dreary, 'So, tell me about yourself!' bit."

You can even spend your bus journey to the date familiarizing yourself with the day's headlines on your smartphone, and picking out a few discussion subjects that will keep things sparky but not too controversial.

Managing Expectations

Once you have your very first date lined up, you might find yourself getting a little overexcited. You'll be standing in the supermarket queue, holding your bottle of wine and a pot of hummus, thinking, "Maybe next time I'm here, I'll be standing with the new love of my life, about to *share* my booze and snacks! Maybe they'll introduce me to a great new brand of crackers! Although, thinking about it, we should definitely get two bottles…" Or you'll buy a straw hat on a spring day, feeling happy and hopeful. "Obviously I can't wear the hat on our first date, that would be a bit weird. But maybe it will go great, and in a few weeks we'll go for a picnic, and I can turn up embodying the spirit of modern vintage! I can make them think that I wear hats all the time, and it's part of my personality!" Wedding invitations are the worst, when you have an "and guest" slot that can be filled in with the face of someone you have yet to meet, and

…you start imagining how they might charm your friends and family, even though they have yet to charm you.

The gap between arranging the first date and the date itself is a joy. It's a romantic holiday, when every thought is scored by a tinkling piano, and every journey you undertake happens in the company of animated, chirping birds that only you can see. And you are encouraged to be as optimistic and cheerful about this as you wish, as long as that hope is tempered by a tiny sense of realism.

Sometimes all the lights are on green, the perfect parking space immediately becomes available, you find what you're looking for in the first shop you visit, and when you reach the cash register, you discover your purchase is on sale. But this sequence of events is rare, and hitting it off with the first person you meet online is rarer still.

By all means, look forward to your date, but think of this as a time in which your body and mind ready themselves for a long period of romantic effort. You don't want to hope so hard that you crumble with disappointment when you discover your date is human, having whipped yourself up into such a frenzy that you were expecting Bionic Angel Jesus. Neither do you want to overlook any major flaws, like alcohol-monitoring ankle tags or County Court Judgements, because you're so dang thrilled to be out on a date that you've let your standards slip to below sea level.

Online, multiple dating is de rigueur but, unless you've discussed it, it's a bit of a buzzkill to get to the third month of your relationship only to discover your new partner is keeping their profile active, and they're not actually disappearing on Tuesday nights to play squash, but we'll come to that later (see Multiple Dating, pages 130–43). When you're going on your first few dates, it's your duty to keep your options so wide open that your brain will think you're at the dentist's. It's the only way you'll be able to keep a sense of perspective.

Maura, a solicitor, explains: "It sounds a bit corny, but the more dating you do, the more you learn about yourself. I came out of a really long-term relationship and started looking online. I was so excited about my first date, and so crushed when the guy turned out to be about as exciting as a traffic jam. But if it had worked out straight away, I wouldn't have discovered what I now know. I've been with my boyfriend for almost a year, and I was quite blasé about our first date, because I'd already been on a few. If I'd have been overly optimistic, he could never have lived up to my expectations, basically because he's a human being!"

> ## I was so excited about my first date, and so crushed when the guy turned out to be about as exciting as a traffic jam.

Worst Date Places Ever

Some say there's no bad place for a date – only bad daters. Those people are wrong. The following venues are guaranteed to leave any potentially perfect romance dead in the water.

Trish, 28:

"He took me to the greyhound races in Wimbledon. It might have been fun but it was a wet, freezing night, and he was so obsessed with gambling that he left me alone to play on the slot machines between races!"

Sasha, 36:

"When we met, he was in the middle of organizing his grandmother's funeral. He asked to meet me at the top of a road, which turned out to be the location of the funeral parlour. I understand why it was convenient for him, but it was still really weird!"

Matt, 29:

"Our first date was a surprise trip to Thorpe Park. The surprise for my date was that just thinking about going on a rollercoaster makes me violently ill."

Eleni, 41:

"He asked me to meet him at his house and, naively, I assumed we'd be going out somewhere. No. We were hanging out with his mum. And it was her birthday."

Jack, 35:

"I still feel bad about this, but my date had booked a table at a very smart restaurant that specialized in shellfish, to which I am horribly allergic. I didn't realize it was a seafood place, and had to run away on arrival when I saw a big crab on someone else's plate."

Chrissie, 32:

"One of the guys I met online was a teacher, and he asked me to come to Parents' Evening. I was tempted to go, just because it was so inappropriate and I thought I might get the chance to tease him in front of his students."

Dean, 39:

"I spent one horribly awkward first date watching a burlesque show with this girl. A dancer got so close to me that she flicked my eye with her nipple tassel and I had to sit there with a fixed grin on my face, feeling as if I was about to go blind."

Caitie, 24:

"The city farm was a lovely date idea, but it didn't really work on a wet, muddy day – especially not after I fell in some unidentified animal poo."

The Five Types of Internet Date

Your first internet date will be one of the scariest, strangest scenarios you'll ever find yourself in, but once you've been on 20 dates, you'll notice that patterns have started to form. These will become oddly familiar and comforting, like the particularly loud floral design on the bedroom curtains of the first flat you rented. It's important not to feel too dispirited at this point – everyone has to endure at least one of each type of date before they find love. It's like the Labours of Hercules – but with more anxious texting. Here's what to watch out for.

The casual coffee

 This is less of a date, more of a compromise, which is over before it begins. The vibe is always too straight, sober and business-y. Neither of you really wants to be there, and you end up talking as if you're both middle managers interviewing each other for an internship that doesn't exist. It ends with a handshake, and when one party has left, the other will linger for a bit, then march up to the coffee shop counter to buy and eat three chocolate brownies.

The never-ender

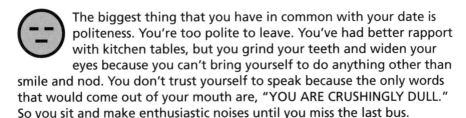 The biggest thing that you have in common with your date is politeness. You're too polite to leave. You've had better rapport with kitchen tables, but you grind your teeth and widen your eyes because you can't bring yourself to do anything other than smile and nod. You don't trust yourself to speak because the only words that would come out of your mouth are, "YOU ARE CRUSHINGLY DULL." So you sit and make enthusiastic noises until you miss the last bus.

The rap date

The greatest symptom of modern malaise is the number of semi-sentient human CVs walking the street. These guys and gals might seem listless, but they've got more lists than a BuzzFeed features meeting: lists of where their clothes came from and how much they cost; lists of their interactions with famous people; lists of their career achievements, from assistant vice-head ice-cream vendor at Splash World to chief photocopier toner operator. But, mainly, it's lists to do with their stuff. Their conversation sounds like an inventory of P. Diddy's car-boot sale table. You will pass out with boredom and never see them again.

The wacky date!

This is never a mutually agreed outing, but the plan of a would-be lothario who thinks he can boost his crazy credentials by taking every potential conquest skydiving. This is in spite of the fact that the skydiving has never, ever, led to a second date. The reluctant guest will do her best to be game and appreciate the wild spirit of the individual, but it will end in actual tears and, possibly, the ejection of other bodily fluids. The skydiver will have nothing to offer conversationally, other than a discussion about the number of planes he has thrown himself out of.

The drinking contest

You will both be sweetly and endearingly nervous. You will then be amazed by how well the conversation flows, once you've finished your first drink. After a couple more, you will both be ready to co-present a late-night underground gonzo comedy show. You will be unbuttoning each other's shirts before one of you says, "Shall we just get a bottle?" You will have one of the best evenings of your life, wake up feeling like you've been eaten by a whale in the night, and vomit on the way to work. You will never see each other again because you're both convinced you did something awful. You didn't.

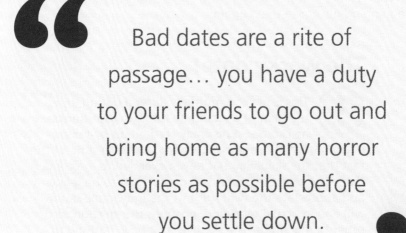

"Bad dates are a rite of passage… you have a duty to your friends to go out and bring home as many horror stories as possible before you settle down."

CHAPTER 6

• • • • • • • • • • • •

Internet Dates From Hell

• • • • • • • • • • • •

The Rite of Passage

It might take a few months, it could be a couple of years, but eventually you will meet someone and end up moving in with them, or marrying them, or both. You will discover someone who seems so right for you it's as if the heavens made them to order, like a human Subway sandwich. Your love life will be a glorious source of joy, and some day, you and your partner will be curled up beside a roaring fire, gently dozing into balloons of vintage brandy, and your mind will drift to the times you spent waiting at a bus stop to meet someone from the internet, only to discover they looked – and smelled – just like Oscar the Grouch. Or the occasion your online date asked to meet you for a romantic summer picnic, and forced you to eat an off-brand pre-packaged pasty on a garage forecourt. And the self-described rollercoaster enthusiast whose profile proclaimed they were an adrenaline junkie, but omitted to say they were liable to vomit on your hair in terror if things got a bit bumpy on the pedalos.

You might shudder at these memories, but you'll smile, too. You'll feel your muscles contract and relax, and your entire body will be flooded with a sudden, pleasurable warmth – a hot-stone massage for the soul. You will feel smugger than you have ever felt before. And that's OK. You have done your time and earned your happiness. When you've been on every single bad date the universe can offer, you're really ready for love. You can smile wryly and roll up your sleeves to show off your battle scars.

Bad dates are a rite of passage. When you start looking for a partner online, you might be picturing dreamy dinners, starlit beaches and parks with parades of ducklings. Your pals, especially the ones who have had a go themselves, see it differently. You now have an obligation of entertainment. You have a duty to your friends to go out and bring home as many horror stories as possible, before you settle down.

Terrible internet dates are a great leveller. It doesn't matter how beautiful, rich or even famous you are, you're not immune. A friend of a friend, who just happens to be a pop star, reveals how his attempt to meet a woman on the internet ended in disaster. "We started talking on Twitter, and I liked her a lot, but when we finally arranged to meet, she was so nervous that she turned up really, really drunk. I mean, not just tipsy – she could barely walk or stand." The pop star is happily coupled up now, but he's still not above dining out on a terrible date story to make his friends giggle.

> " *Terrible internet dates are a great leveller. It doesn't matter how beautiful, rich or even famous you are, you're not immune.* "

It's a Laughing Matter

There's no magic formula when it comes to meeting "the one". Think of it as a computer game with no cheats, no hacks and no Easter eggs that will help you skip 17 levels and grab your Prince or Princess Peach. You just need to keep plodding through and meeting each new challenge with a nod and a giggle. And you *will* score points. The more people you meet, the more you'll learn, making you the best partner that you can be when the time is right. Just keep laughing and remember that you're not alone. As long as stories like these can raise a smile, there's hope.

It's all relative

Family has no place on a first date, but that didn't stop these aspiring romantics from aiming for a vibe that was, quite frankly, slightly incestuous…

Eleni, 28:

"At first I thought it was quite cute that the guy messaging me claimed to feel really comfortable around women because he was the youngest in his family and had three big sisters. But on the date, they were all he talked about. I mean, he barely spoke about his own career, but he spent a solid half-hour describing his sisters' various job searches and promotions. He even complimented me on my dress, saying, 'It looks like something one of my sisters would wear.' Then he complained about the fact that none of his sisters wanted to go on holiday with him. I suspect they were as weirded out by their brother as I was!"

Tia, 34:

"Our very first date was going fine until he said, 'When you meet my mum, you'll have to do something about all that make-up. She doesn't like painted women.' At first I laughed; I thought he was being really deadpan. When it turned out he was completely serious, I paid the bill and said I had an early meeting. Luckily, I did end up meeting someone great, and the woman who is now my mother-in-law is completely awesome and wouldn't care if I turned up at her house looking like RuPaul."

Misha, 31:

"He asked me to meet him at a nearby bar for a quick drink before we went for dinner. He did not tell me that his family was having some kind of mini reunion in the bar. When he introduced me to everyone as 'that girl I've been telling you about,' I felt a bit panicky. I mean, at that point we hadn't ever met before, and I thought we were just getting to know each other – I hadn't mentioned him to anyone beyond saying I had a date that night. Then his 80-year-old uncle went to kiss my hand and started to suck my fingers! Everyone laughed and said, 'Oh, you'll have to watch that Eddie, he's got a real thing for young ladies,' but I was just horribly grossed out and wanted to run home to bleach my hand. I couldn't think of a polite way to leave, so I stayed and had a drink with the guy. We got to sit at our own table but the relatives just stared at us throughout. I told him I had a migraine, bailed on dinner and avoided his messages. I should have told him he was making me feel uncomfortable – at least I could have saved another poor girl the same experience!"

Minding Your Table Manners

Because you can tell a lot about someone from the way they wield a fork.

Jessamy, 30:

"To be honest, I was a little bit disappointed when my date picked a ubiquitous pizza chain for our first date. I mean, that's fine for a gossipy lunch with girlfriends, but it's not very romantic. I didn't want him to spend a lot of money, but I was hoping he'd go for something quirkier. But the online chat had been really fun, so I gave him the benefit of the doubt. All became clear when we arrived and he presented our waiter with a sheaf of money-off vouchers and printed coupons. Again, it was a bit of a turn-off, but I told myself to stop being so shallow. The final straw came when we tried to order, and when I said what I wanted, he shouted, 'You can't have that! It's not in the offer!' I was totally thrown and said I'd pay the extra, but he claimed that would invalidate the fact that he had chosen from the special, cheap menu. Then he threw his napkin at me and stormed off into the night. The waiter watched him reach the other side of the street, then burst out laughing and brought me a glass of champagne. If it had been a movie, I'd have ended up with the waiter, but he said I reminded him of his single daughter who had similar dating horror stories."

Hattie, 35:

"The weirdest online date I ever had was with a guy who ate my food. I was really excited because we had both been messaging about our favourite restaurants, and I thought that we had loads in common because we were both really into eating. When he started to eat off my plate, I thought he was just being curious and playful. When he continued to do it, I felt a little annoyed. And when, with his mouth full of my food, he said, 'Why did you even order this celeriac? It's awful,' I decided to leave. I stopped for a McDonald's on the way home."

Selina, 27:

"I met an older guy online, and really wasn't worried about the age gap, until he started trying to feed me. We were in a really fancy restaurant, one I'd dreamed about going to for months, and when my food arrived, he snatched it off me, loaded his spoon with it and did the 'here-comes-the-aeroplane' thing, complete with sound effects. I was so shocked I couldn't open my mouth, so he sort of forced the spoon inside. When I said I was a little uncomfortable with that, he sulked, ironically like a three-year-old. He actually stopped talking. I left before dessert."

The Not-So-Great Outdoors

The following anecdotes illustrate why nearly all dates take place in bars. You can't get chased by a dog in a bar. Well, it's unlikely.

Cecilia, 23:

"To be fair, this was not my date's fault. He proposed a picnic, and packed champagne, cake, spendy dips – you know, everything that could possibly make outdoor dining fabulous. I was wearing a white floaty dress, he had a linen shirt on, and it all looked too good to be true. It was. Just as I was about to bite into my first sandwich, I almost swallowed a wasp. It stung me on the lips, and the pain was agonizing, and as I was flailing around and trying to get it off me, I rolled into a pile of poo. I'm assuming it came from a dog, but who knows? My lips were enormous and I was covered in brown stains. My date kindly offered to take me to the hospital, but the whole thing was a bit of a buzzkill. After we'd waited in there for a few hours, he apologized and told me he had to leave because he had another date that evening!"

Nina, 32:

"Stupidly, I'd written a load of stuff in my profile that claimed I was really sporty and up for an adventure. If I'm entirely honest, my occasional gym habit doesn't make me sporty or adventurous. So when a really hot, athletic guy started messaging me, I was very focused on how sexy he was and not really thinking about how we had absolutely nothing in common. He invited me to go on a date with him and made a really big deal about how he had planned this exciting 'surprise'. It was paintballing. We were put on opposing teams, so we didn't really get to talk at all. He was running around, screaming, having the time of his life, while I hid behind a tree and cried. I never saw him again, but I did find an awesome guy, who likes more sedate activities, once I'd changed my profile and made it a little bit more honest."

Aurelie, 27:

" We had an informal first date – a quick coffee and a walk in the park – and, if I'm honest, I was a little bored. He was really sparky and funny online, but in real life he didn't have much to say for himself. That all changed when he spotted a family playing with their dog. The dog was off its leash, and he went on this tirade about how irresponsible it was, how it should be illegal, someone might get hurt – he sounded a little crazy. Then the dog, thinking the angry, arm-waving man was a new friend, started to chase him. My date bolted across the park and ended up climbing a tree. I'm sorry to say that I wasn't able to help him out – I was laughing too hard. Now I know that not being a dog lover isn't a deal breaker, but a guy should be able to appreciate a cute puppy! "

50 Ways [Approximately] To Leave Your Lover

When you're on a nightmare date, there will come a point at which it's only logical to take off and abandon all attempts to rescue your evening. But how do you do this without hurting anyone's feelings? How can you break it to your date that you would rather be at home with your TV? The following techniques are not recommended, owing to physical and emotional safety issues, but they are effective.

● ●

It's Over!

✖ Disappear in a puff of smoke – keep a box of baby powder in your bag and use it as a temporary cloak to obscure your exit.

✖ Flash a police badge and say, "I'm sorry, I guess you're not the suspect I'm looking for after all. Have a nice evening."

✖ Go on a TV prop-making course and learn how to create fake vomit. Deploy fake vomit when the dinner conversation becomes unbearable.

✖ Pretend that you're hosting a hidden camera show, and ask them to sign a model-release form.

✖ Get off with the waiter.

✖ If they ask what you want to do on your next date, ask to go shoplifting.

✖ Bring a rolled-up rope ladder with you and use it to sneak out of the bathroom window.

✖ Play dead.

✖ Tell them you can't wait to have children together and enter them into beauty pageants.

✖ Pretend to be on fire. Stop, drop and roll. Roll all the way home without saying goodbye. They'll get the message.

✖ Think about what happened in *Jurassic Park* – if you stay very still, the dinosaurs can't see you. So stop moving and hope that your date thinks you've already left.

✖ Ask your date to go in on a timeshare with you, but say they have to sign the cheque tonight in order to take advantage of the low, low prices.

✖ Text a friend and bribe them to dress up as a wolf and attack your date, while you sneak off.

✖ Suggest a look around the nearest camping shop. Hide in one of the tents until your date goes home.

✖ They will be suspicious if you say you need to go and check on your cat, so add detail. Say that the last time you left the house, your cat grew thumbs, ordered £500 worth of pizza and started sending porn video links to everyone in your email address book.

✖ In a restaurant? Throw some food at the person at the next table, and then tell the waiter that your date did it. They'll get thrown out straight away.

✖ Offer them one of your kidneys. Say you're looking for a four-figure fee, but you'll give them a mates' rates discount.

✖ Look them in the eye and say that you've just realized you might be their first cousin.

Play Dead

Ultimately, remember
that you owe it to
yourself and your date
to break it off if it
doesn't feel right.

CHAPTER 7

• • • • • • • • • • • • •

Selection and Rejection

• • • • • • • • • • • •

Saying Yes, Saying No

To be good at online dating, you need the unshakeable confidence and tenacity of a door-to-door salesperson whose job it is to sell internet users a new service that relies on old tin cans and bits of string. You will get rejected, more than once, and it will be horrible. You'll find yourself invoking and inverting the old Groucho Marx quote, and deciding that the less people want to have you in their club, the more desperate you are to, at least, get a glimpse of their members. And when your messages are ignored and your dates don't turn up, there's a chance you'll start to feel bitter, or at least take the opportunity to wield the power that has, so far, been used against you. There is no one pickier than the person who has been scorned so many times that they decide to take revenge on the entire romantic community by replying, "EWWW! NO THANK YOU!" in 72-point capitals to anyone who asks them if they'd like to go bowling.

Objectively, you know that you can't second-guess anyone's motives – they might have received your message on the day they got back with their ex, or heard their work was moving them to Australia, or decided to take religious orders. If they did look at your picture and think, "Not for me," there's every chance that your face didn't bother them but your sweater reminded them of a psychotic schoolteacher who tortured the class stick insect to death. There's nothing you can do here, other than stay a little bit fatalistic for your own sanity. On the other hand, you're going to receive plenty of messages that are, at best, bafflingly presumptuous, leaving you with no desire to date the sender. (Rest assured that your own messages are not having this effect on anyone, unless you are spamming every match within a 50-mile radius with "DTF?" and a picture of your genitals.) If the power of refusal hasn't made you cruel, there's a possibility you might find yourself struggling with a different extreme, saying "yes" to everyone because you're an empathic soul and you know rejection makes people sad.

Essentially, no matter which guidelines you are given, you will probably end up going your own way and learning from it. And there's nothing wrong with that. The only real mistake you can make is to think you're developing skills that only apply in the dating world. Even if you meet "The One" in a matter of months, the period leading up to it will make you more observant, reactive and tactical than Ronaldo himself. You'll be able to take on any amount of awkward workplace negotiations once you've given, and received, a little virtual romantic pain. At the very least, you'll be tough enough to sit through your appraisal with a smile on your face, and strong enough to get the intern to stop stealing pens.

> " ...you're going to receive plenty of messages that are, at best, bafflingly presumptuous, leaving you with no desire to date the sender. "

There's No Reply

Your idiot correspondent has wasted many an awkward evening on dating sites "letting people down gently, so as to be polite", and not because she is a Glinda the Good Witch figure, inundated with suitors, who feels she needs to do right by them because she is as kind as she is beautiful. Rather, it's because she is hopelessly English and had been attempting online dating for a whole month before she realized most sites supply you with a polite "No thanks" button.

If you've been nicely or "Britishly" brought up, it might seem alarmingly rude to completely ignore anyone who has taken the time to talk to you, but if you immediately get a bored vibe or bad feeling from their message, it's the kindest thing to do. Most people will see any kind of response as an encouragement, and before too long your dating admin will become more traumatic than your work admin, and you'll be typing through gritted teeth, thinking you'd rather be emailing a persistent sales rep to say you're still happy with your printer paper supplier but if that ever changes, they will be the first to know.

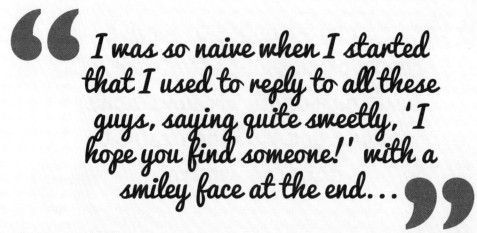

I was so naive when I started that I used to reply to all these guys, saying quite sweetly, 'I hope you find someone!' with a smiley face at the end...

When you've been online for a little while, you'll develop a sixth sense for the messages that are essentially spam, and you'll stop bothering with those too. Most of the time, it's immediately obvious, but occasionally you'll be taken in by something that sounds quite normal, only to realize it's a dazzling triumph of copy-and-paste over content. Remember, the rules online are much like those of the streets and bars. If someone approaches you and you ignore them, that is their cue to leave you alone. Should they persist, that is harassment, and there will be a function or app that allows you to report them to the administrators. You don't owe anyone anything, and maintaining a strict policy in which you only reply to users you like will make sure you can keep everything light and fun.

Grace, a beauty therapist, says:

"I was so naive when I started that I used to reply to all these guys, saying quite sweetly, 'I hope you find someone!' with a smiley face at the end, even when it was clear that the only thing we had in common was that we were both single and on a dating site. Initially, you have this misguided sense of community, where you feel you want to be nice to everyone because you're all in the same boat. But I don't think karma exists online. I'd get persistent creepy messages from the people I'd declined, just because I'd bothered to reply – but I didn't get any polite, cheerful refusals from any of the guys I'd messaged who weren't into me! I guess manners and standards are a bit different, and expectations are lower. Once you've worked that out, it gets much easier."

When Brutal Honesty Is the Best Policy

The awkward, painful business of rejection doesn't end online –
it will, almost inevitably, need to happen face-to-face too, which is a process
that even the most committed sadomasochist would struggle to find enjoyable.
If there is an upside, this does make it a bit easier to turn people down at the
messaging stage before you're acquainted with their coffee preferences and
personal odour.

Depending on whom you're asking, at least one in four of your early dates will be with
someone you want to run away from before you've even sat down. So how much
misery is a person expected to withstand before they bolt? Beth, a biologist, reckons it's
always worth giving someone the benefit of the doubt. "Admittedly, when your heart
sinks and you think, 'Oh, goodness me, no,' your instincts are usually bang on. But for
the sake of kindness and human decency, if you've agreed to meet someone, I think
you owe them at least 15 minutes of chat, or as long as it takes for you to drink a cup
of tea." Her friend Suzie agrees. "Occasionally I've been proved wrong and ended up
having a really lovely time with someone I've not been sure about initially. It's rare, but
basically you don't want to come away thinking 'what if…'. Should the worst come to
the worst, and sometimes it does, you'll have a funny story."

So there's a minimum amount of time for which one is obliged to sit through a bad
date – but is there also a maximum? Cara says, "If I could give anyone any advice about
bad dates, I would say, 'If you want to leave, leave.' Nothing is more grim than wanting

Take a deep breath...

Nothing is more grim than wanting to cry with misery and boredom when you're halfway through a starter, but you stay put because you've got a steak coming.

to cry with misery and boredom when you're halfway through a starter, but you stay put because you've got a steak coming. And you don't need to be polite – well, always be polite, but don't lie. Take a deep breath, tell them you don't think you're hitting it off and then leave. Don't apologize, don't explain and don't forget to pay for anything you've eaten or had to drink." According to Greek legend, Persephone got stuck in the underworld for inadvertently enjoying the hospitality of the devilish Hades. You don't want to get trapped in a hell of your own making because you owe someone called Darren a fiver for olives and you think there's a chance he has glowing horns under his baseball cap.

We're all very familiar with the litany of cat- and oven-based excuses that single people employ when on dates. However horrible your companion is, it simply doesn't do to throw a cliché in their face. And never assume they're perceptive enough to take a hint. Ria, a party planner, reveals, "I've used every excuse in the book to get out of bad dates, and every time I'll get an email afterwards that says, 'It's a shame you had to leave for that emergency meeting with your landlady/last-minute catch-up with your boss/gas leak. Let's do it again soon!' I'm only getting their messages because they're not getting mine. You have to spell it out."

Calling It a Day

Of course, once you've been out a few times, letting someone down gently feels about as feasible as tipping a warm, sleeping puppy out of a cushioned basket into a cold cage of cats. But sometimes it takes a few dates to make your mind up, and it's important to stay focused and remember what you want and why you're looking for love online. All too often, ease and familiarity let a less-than-great relationship get off the ground because it's easy to confuse the path to true love with the slow slide towards cosiness and comfort.

• • • • • • • • • • • • • • • • • • •

Etta, an actress, says:

"It sounds brutal but sometimes the best way to work out what someone is really like is to wait until the third or fourth date, because that's when a person starts to relax and let their guard down. Initially, they're going to be on their best behaviour, but when they've learned to chill out around you, you might find that they're really rude to waiters, or they're not naturally good listeners, or just that they have some unfortunate but annoying tic or habit that basically you couldn't bear to live with."

"

...very few of the people you meet will be right for you in a forever-and-ever sort of sense....

"

Carrie, a designer, adds:

"You have to keep thinking of it as a job interview – but one where, weirdly, you're both interviewing each other for the same gig. If you were interviewing for a major role, you'd expect to go through a few rounds, and this is the same thing. Make sure you maintain a little bit of distance and keep a clear head."

This is not to say you shouldn't have fun, but remember that dating sometimes creates its own kinetic energy, and after a frustrating lack of matches, the fun of having a few cocktails with someone who is able to speak in complete sentences can mean you get carried away.

If you've met at least twice and you're not feeling it, you do owe your date a reasonably thorough explanation. Make sure you are as clear and honest as possible, but be kind too. Heidi, a PR consultant, says, "I've been in that situation a few times, and it's not always easy to be specific. But focus on your incompatibility, rather than delivering a clumsy character assassination. If you both spend your weekends playing or watching completely different sports, or one of you travels a lot for work, or you're at opposite ends of the political spectrum – well, that's easier for someone to hear than, 'Sorry, I like you, but you smell a bit weird.'"

Ultimately, remember that you owe it to yourself and your date to break things off if it doesn't feel right. And very few of the people you meet will be right for you in a forever-and-ever sort of sense, but most won't be so freaky you can't face having a single drink with them. You'll encounter many three-date wonders, and that's what makes the search so wonderful when you finally find the one you want.

What to Do When It's You, Not Them

Obviously, it would be crazy to claim that you're going to be the one doing all the rejecting. You are not the ruler of Internet Love Land, and unless you're a glutton for punishment, it's much harder to hear that you're the one with the problem. Even the most cheerful, confident people get rejected, and they think it sucks. Etta says, "When I started dating, I thought I was completely ready for the onslaught of nasty messages and no-shows. I audition all the time, and for each occasion I get the job, there are at least eight or nine goes where I fail horribly. But if I'm going to keep paying my rent and eating, I just need to keep picking myself up and going back in there. So how hard could dating be? As it turns out, really hard!"

Etta believes that learning to deal with a new form of rejection hasn't been pleasant, but it has helped her get better at her job. "It might be a cliché, but it's true. Adversity does make you stronger. When someone criticizes my hair, face or voice and uses it as a reason not to date me, it breaks my heart, but it means I find it much easier to hear it as a reason for people not to hire me! Then, usually all I've lost out on is a shampoo or butter commercial."

Carrie thinks it's important to remember that you can never know the agenda of the person who's rejecting you. "A good friend married a guy she met through a dating site, and so when I signed up I was really optimistic, and I just hadn't prepared myself for the amount of rejection and negativity I ended up hearing. But my friend said she'd been through it, and explained that many of the people who use dating sites have just come

"You have to keep picking yourself up, dusting yourself down and going back to work.

out of bad relationships or are frustrated about being single, and that can have a really bad effect on their interactions."

Carrie's point is that if anyone does go out of their way to make you feel bad when they're saying no, that's their problem – and if they're that mean to a total stranger, you absolutely don't want to end up dating them anyway. The toughest thing about rejection is that it can dent your confidence and make it that much harder to keep going. Carrie's idea is a great one. Never be afraid to tell your friends when online dating is getting a bit much. If you've got an awkward rejection story, your closest pals can easily rustle up 50 in a matter of minutes. When you realize that it doesn't matter how gorgeous, funny, clever, wealthy or hot someone is, they can still find rejection crushing, you'll feel your own confidence start to creep back. Etta's attitude is exactly the right one. You have to keep picking yourself up, dusting yourself down and going back to work.

Parting Shots

For some reason, the act of dating dismissal makes everyone believe they are Lord Byron or, at the very least, someone who has just won a comedy award. More often than not, wit is no substitute for empathy, and even more often than that, there's no wit to speak of. But reading a collection of the worst-ever exit lines is a great way to cheer yourself up when you're licking your wounds and sulking into your rioja. Here's the best of the worst, and the worst of the worst.

Helene, 33, vet:

"A guy actually told me he had to end it because he was married to the sea. Seriously, that's a Homer Simpson line. He did like sailing, to be fair, but I wasn't impressed. I suspect that one was for the best."

Danni, 36, writer:

"One guy gave me an ultimatum and said that he'd leave me if I didn't get a boob job. So I told him that he'd better leave me. He was a club promoter and I think he was more interested in going out with someone who would fit an image he had in his head than someone he actually got on with."

Cecilia, 24, student:

"I once heard 'Babe, there is no "u" in "future".' I told him there were two "u's" and walked away. Amazingly, he was studying English."

Caterina, 38, dentist:

"A guy broke it off because he wasn't sure about my aura. I should have tried to look upset but I couldn't stop laughing."

Hata, 22, gymnast:

"It was the classic, 'I love you, but I'm not in love with you. I think of you as a sister.' What made it worse was that we'd just finished having sex."

Christina, 29, doctor:

"He told me he couldn't be bothered with the distance, when we lived at either end of the same city. I hope he has fun hooking up with his next-door neighbour, who, I happen to know, is an 84-year-old man."

Olu, 40, accountant:

"She said that, during a date, she was thinking about climbing out of the window and escaping from the pub, but realized it was probably better for her to come down the stairs like a normal person and tell me how she was feeling. I don't know. I think I'd rather still be in the pub, drunk and confused, than hear that."

Ben, 30, fitness instructor:

"It was brutal. She said, 'I've been having a think and I've decided that I never, ever want you to meet my family.' Let's face it, it wasn't going to go anywhere after that."

Tracie, 35, personal trainer:

"He said that we were astrologically incompatible because I'm a Taurus and he's a Virgo, and he was fundamentally too sexually intense for me."

He or she who dares to date everyone wins. There are no prizes for waiting.

CHAPTER 8

· · · · · · · · · · · · · · · ·

Multiple Dating

· · · · · · · · · · · · · ·

Into the Dating Pool

At first, your dating inbox might resemble an old, dusty town in nineteenth-century California, after the Gold Rush. You'll wonder if you accidentally downloaded a tumbleweed screensaver – tumbleweed that pauses on its journey across the page to whisper, "Even I wouldn't have sex with you, and I am made of pixels!" Then, just when your self-esteem couldn't plummet any lower and you've filled up an Etsy shopping basket with "Crochet your own boyfriend" kits, it will happen. There will be a dribble, then a trickle, then a wave of sexy new single people desperate to make your acquaintance, filling your computer with emoticons, invitations and alarmingly saucy suggestions.

This period can be as overwhelming as it is exciting. When it's all quiet on the dating front, you can pull the comforting duvet of self-pity closer and order another pizza. But when you're getting more action than a GI Joe doll on a reconnaissance mission to Barbie's pool house, it's easy to lose your head, even if it isn't made of moulded plastic.

The first thing to do is enjoy it! Give yourself a pat on the head or perhaps walk with a little shimmy next time you're on the way to the bathroom. You're hot stuff, and the people of the internet are right to be interested. Of course they should want to date you! You would.

Next, you must invest in some kind of organizational app or device (if you live for all things retro, by all means use a Filofax), because you've got a lot of dating to do and, sadly, it's not going to be as spontaneous as it looks in the movies. Plot and plan carefully, otherwise you could end up arriving a day early for pizza with Paul, and manage to miss the screening of *Arachnophobia* that you were supposed to attend

> *But when you're getting more action than a GI Joe doll on a reconnaissance mission to Barbie's pool house, it's easy to lose your head...*

with Alphonse. Also, in the movies, everyone loves a scatterbrain, but in real life, they lose phones, house keys and, eventually, jobs and friends. It might be a bit of a shock, depending on the dating culture you're used to, but if you're going to find someone online, you have to be up for dating a different person every night. Well, maybe not quite that frequently, because you'll be exhausted, but aim for three or four times a week. Do it instead of the gym – it's much more fun.

Even if you detest drama, there's no point approaching the dating process sedately. Your matches won't wait to meet you one at a time. Let's suppose you start by forsaking all others for Paul, only to discover, two months in, that he's obsessed with watching reruns of *Robot Truck Wars* and has a whole 14 albums of Facebook pictures entitled "Ladbantz: Volumes I–XIV". In the meantime, Alphonse might have met someone else, and he won't be single until after you start, misguidedly, dating an anally retentive conceptual trapeze artist called Horaldo. He, or she, who dares to date everyone, wins. There are no prizes for waiting.

Rules and Guidelines

Multiple dating becomes much easier once you learn that everyone is doing the same thing as you. There's a code of conduct that varies slightly, depending on the match and the site where you met them, but it means that everyone can be upfront and honest without needing to provide a new date with a spreadsheet of exactly whom they have been seeing, complete with an algorithm that dictates designated date venues – "I'm sorry, I've already been for coffee this week. That means you have to take me for steak!"

Don't talk about exes, but do talk about your online dating experiences. If you've been on a few weird dates, it can be a good bonding topic, and there's no point shying away from the subject that has brought you both together in the first place. However, you don't need to list the potential lovers you've already met, or the people you've encountered and hope to see again. A bad date is a fabulous anecdote, but the great date you went on yesterday will destroy the potentially wonderful one you're on today, if you talk about it.

> "...often, you'll encounter someone who does not know how the game is played and thinks it works a little like Top Trumps.

Breakfast - Lunch
Coffee - Dinner
?

With that in mind, watch out for any dodgy date chat from your brand new friend. Most of the time, they will know the rules and understand that it's bad manners to start listing their recent successes and conquests. However, every so often, you'll encounter someone who does not know how the game is played and thinks it works a little like Top Trumps: listing scores of potential partners gives them points for success and desirability. This is the hallmark of an idiot, and they'll get over it one day, but not on your watch. Give them a wide berth.

However, do remember that if you find your date charming and charismatic, you're probably not the only one. Successful multiple dating means managing your expectations. Do your best to reserve judgement on the first date, and you'll feel fairly relaxed when the second comes along. If you imagine yourself to have fallen in love at first sight, you're going to be pretty miserable when you check your messages and see that their profile is still getting plenty of attention.

Ultimately, the most important rule of all is the "job interview" one. No one, date or otherwise, cares about your fabulous personality or collection of hilarious stories if you fail to manage the basic human requirements and don't turn up on time and clean. When people have packed dating schedules, they don't want to be waiting for half an hour, watching their coffee get cold and wondering where you are, because you did your ditzy free-spirit thing and got on the wrong bus. For your own sanity, arrange dates in areas where no one has to worry about anything boring like car parking or transport links. When you're seeing someone who is on their eighth date of the week, you don't want to be remembered as the woman who made them take a really expensive taxi ride.

Keeping Your Cool

We all have shameful stories about how, when dating, we've been a little less relaxed than we would have liked.

• •

Katherine, an administrator, admits:

"I wasn't even really dating this guy properly – we were seeing each other – but when he got up to leave after a few beers, I told him I was wearing matching underwear and shouted, 'Please come back to mine! It's Valentine's Day tomorrow!' Since then, multiple dating has really sorted out my sense of perspective. I could get a little bit intense, and this way I'm not focusing all my energy on one man."

If you've been single for a while, dating a wide range of people can be a great confidence boost, but it also helps you to stop taking the dating scene quite so seriously. When you've spent a long time wailing about how hard it is to meet people, it can be a bit of a shock when you realize it can't be that hard because you've met 20 people in the last month. Being single can feel isolating, as it's easy to spend all your time focusing on what is absent from your life, rather than looking at what you do have. You might feel that everyone around you is coupled up because you're zeroing in on relationships. So being around other single people might just make you feel less anxious about meeting someone. Even if you don't fancy anyone you meet at the moment, you've now got a gang to belong to.

Multiple dating tends to expose the way we mythologize and fetishize love, and makes us realize how unhelpful that is. Meeting someone that you want to spend the rest of your life with is supposed to be a freakishly impossible feat. You want the love that can only be found in books, songs and movies. You want it to be difficult because it is valued so heavily. But there's no mystery or magic to it. Dating is about volume and numbers. It's not romance, it's ro-maths. Once you've cracked that code, you're less likely to lose your mind because you're worried that you've met the one and only and they might not love you back. It's easier to stay calm and keep things casual, and if it doesn't work out, onto the next one. And remember, the people you meet and don't want to settle down with might enhance your life in other ways. Janie, a reporter, says, "I went on two dates with this guy back in 2010, before I met my boyfriend, and we became Facebook friends. He was not the love of my life but, when I was looking for removals people, he did help me to move house!"

> **When you've spent a long time wailing about how hard it is to meet people, it can be a bit of a shock when you realize it can't be that hard because you've met 20 people in the last month.**

The Thrill of the Kiss

If someone judges you for having coffee with three different people in as many days, they might be a time traveller from the Edwardian era. But is it different if the coffee date is taking place in your flat and, erm, you don't have any clothes on? Even in these liberated days, there are a few different opinions floating about regarding how intimate you allow yourself to get when you're dating more than one person. As long as everyone is consenting and happy, there are basically no rules. But it will come up, and it's always best to be as prepared as a boy scout, if only so you don't end up spending more on condoms than the average monthly mortgage payment.

● ● ● ● ● ● ● ● ● ● ● ● ● ● ● ● ● ●

Shoshanna, 32, says:

"When I first started seeing people, it was all part of the fun. I'd usually end up hooking up with my dates, because... well, who doesn't like kissing?" However, Shoshanna reckons that, depending on what you're into, the fun isn't sustainable. "Basically, I had a bit of a scare. Everything was fine in the end, but I forgot to use protection one time and had a little panic. I realized it wasn't just about birth control. It's hard to regulate exactly what you're exposing yourself to health-wise, when you end up sleeping with everyone you date." Shoshanna says that, as far as she's concerned, the only rule is to do what makes you feel comfortable and happy. "When I was a bit more casual about things, I had so much fun, but the fairly rational worries that came with it eventually made me think that it wasn't right for me. It was a bit like loving chocolate but knowing it was better for me to have a tiny bit every so often, instead of stuffing my face with it every day and wondering why I had an upset stomach."

Who doesn't like Kissing?

Lana, 35, adds:

"It's important to remember that most people will not reject you romantically because you refused to sleep with them, or because you did sleep with them. If that does happen (and the majority of us will experience it from a minority of asshats), it's because the person doing it is absolutely not worth dating, and it's brilliant that you found out sooner rather than later. Sex can mean everything, or nothing, but it usually falls somewhere between the two poles. If you sleep with a date who lets you down, and you feel a bit emotional and weird about it afterwards, don't worry. Millions of people have the same experience, and it won't stop you from living the cool, single-person dream. Similarly, if you're having a wide variety of casual, carefree hook-ups and people say snide, outdated things about cows and free milk, it's your life and they can jog on. Just tell them all your lovers are allergic to dairy".

The only non-negotiable if you're going to enjoy the physical side of multiple dating or, indeed, any dating, is condoms. There is no safe sex, only safer sex. Neither age and experience, nor youth and stupidity, will protect you from disease. If you're seeing multiple partners, you're multiplying your risk. Wrap up the goods before you leave the store.

Counting Woes

The best thing about multiple dating is that it increases the number of hilariously awkward stories that you'll end up telling all your friends. Here are some of our faves:

Elizabeth, 26:

"I'd been on an OK date with a guy I met online on a Tuesday night, and someone else I'd just started seeing through the website picked the same venue for the following Thursday. Of course, the original guy was in there and saw us kissing. He was staring into my eyes just as I pulled away. The barman thought this was so funny that he had a glass of champagne sent to me by the 'handsome gentleman in the corner'. Luckily, Thursday Night Guy laughed, otherwise I might have cried."

Cathy, 24:

"When I tried speed dating, I'd already been on dates with about five of the guys in there. It was really depressing, especially as two of them didn't recognize me! Still, it ended up giving me something to talk about with a few of the other potential dates, and I left with some phone numbers. All was not lost!"

Charlie, 32:

"Only I could end up pulling sodding housemates. I'd hooked up with one when rather drunk, and when the other one took me back to his place a few days later, I couldn't quite believe it when he brought me to the same building. Neither could the first housemate, who was eating toast in his pants on the sofa when I walked in for the second time."

Jessie, 29:

"I accidentally pursued the same guy on four different dating sites. His pictures were all slightly different, and I wasn't paying that much attention, but he did eventually ask me if I was some kind of stalker. I pointed out that his ages were different on every site, which didn't go down too well. Since then I've decided that I'm happy to date a few guys at the same time, but I'm only going to look for them in one place!"

The internet is responsible for millions of matches but they don't all happen on dedicated dating sites.

CHAPTER 9

• • • • • • • • • • • • • •

Unlikely Dating Spots

• • • • • • • • • • • • •

Broaden Your Horizons

The internet is responsible for millions of matches, but they don't all happen on dedicated dating sites. Social networks aren't just the domain of existing smug couples who live to fill our feeds with irritating pictures of their own loved-up faces. They can also generate more flirting opportunities than a Hollywood hot tub on Ashton Kutcher's front lawn.

If you're really focused on starting a serious relationship, though, you'll need to sign up to a proper dating site. Hoping to find something that specific on a social network or elsewhere online is like being desperate for a plumber to fix your bathroom but refusing to call one you found in the *Yellow Pages*. Instead, you stand in the middle of the street, shouting "Who wants to talk to me about taps?!" However, the flirting and dating skills you're learning can definitely be put to good use on Facebook, Twitter and the rest. You'll be more attuned to reading other people's comments and messages, checking for chemistry and analyzing whether you've stumbled upon something worth pursuing.

When you readjust your focus away from the more intense dating scene – relaxing by talking to your friends, catching up on the headlines and searching for pictures of hamsters in sunglasses – the pressure is off. You're taking a break from the frenetic rush to set up dates and you stop worrying constantly about whether you're coming across as the funniest, sexiest, most perfect person with a profile, which, ironically, usually makes you feel funnier and sexier straight away.

Other spaces on the internet also allow you to assess potential love interests with greater accuracy. A dating profile is going to contain a few lies, half-truths and blatant fibs about gym regimes and intellectual abilities. An impressive-sounding profile might leave you cold, because it's clearly written as an advertisement by a person who has a misguided idea of what other users want to see and hear. That person might be far more appealing on social media with a genuine, lively, connected conversation about the joys of baby back ribs and *Ren & Stimpy*. When people are posting regular updates about their lives, you have a much stronger sense of who they are and what they spend their days doing.

The nature of the internet means that dating chat can be a little less stilted than it sometimes gets on a dedicated site. The way we communicate in other places online better reflects real-life conversation. You avoid the temptation to send each other super-detailed, thousand-word messages and end up embracing the rapid-fire, energy-filled, funny, flowing discussions. And you can quickly work out whether you have complementary conversation styles. If you'd like someone who speaks slowly and comes up with measured responses, you'll know it will never work out with someone who can only talk in puppy GIFs. Essentially, using a non-dedicated dating site to find love can be a little like searching for lost keys. As soon as you chill out and stop throwing your sofa cushions around the room, you may discover that what you're looking for isn't where you expected to find it, but right in front of you.

How Does It Work?

Your dedicated dating correspondent has been on a couple – OK, over 30 – dates with people she met on Twitter. And it all worked out so well that she's now living with one of them, and looking at September weddings. Twitter works because it's like going to your best friend's brother's birthday party. You know a couple of people who set up introductions, charming strangers join in with the conversation, and you end the night in the middle of a conga line with 100 new pals. Or you get stuck talking to a commercial vehicles insurance expert with chronic halitosis and racist tendencies, and you're so traumatized by the experience that you can't go to another social gathering for 18 months or more. At least when you're online, it's easier to virtually walk away – or block, report or just stop replying.

> Facebook requires an introduction, but it's a brilliant way to build in a flirt if you've just met someone you liked, but didn't have the time or the opportunity to get to know them. . .

For the most part, everyone is up for a chat, and you've always got something to talk about. It's a space for everyone to share their work and opinions, so the potential conversation topics are laid out in front of you. Also, you might not feel comfortable approaching a hot stranger in a bar and whispering, "I was eavesdropping on your conversation about liberal values in the music of the 1970s and I think you're really fascinating. Let's talk." But that's the mechanism on which Twitter is based, and you can still do it when you're in your pyjamas and your hair is filthy.

Facebook requires an introduction, but it's a brilliant way to build in a flirt if you've just met someone you liked, but didn't have the time or the opportunity to get to know them properly. The Messenger element means it's perfectly acceptable to ping them to say, "Hey", without the pressure that comes with just winking at someone on a site like Match.com. **Instagram** is a more visual version of Twitter, and you can make it work in the same way by leaving likes and flirty comments under people's pictures. It can be very useful for meeting people with a specific interest; say, art or design, or enhancing how you're already interacting with someone on another site. An app called **Jazzed** fuses Instagram's features with a matchmaking facility and aims to help photographers find love.

It's no coincidence that the emerging dating services are borrowing the best features from social media and other elements of the web, and streamlining the way we meet and interact with each other. It means there's a good chance that you're already signed up to a site or service that you can use to meet someone. It might not have "dating" in the name, but if you start thinking of every new person you encounter as a possibility, you'll be using the whole of the web to run your love life.

Social Media Management

If you're going to open up your search and include the whole of the internet, you might have to do a little light social spring-cleaning. This isn't about making drastic changes, but tweaking any available information about you so that it shows you in the best light. That means making sure any Facebook photos of you vomiting into a trash can have been untagged and getting rid of any snarky subtweets or Facebook statuses about how much you hate your neighbours' kid/boss's dog/gynaecologist. Start by showing the world your best self, and then you can figure out who gets to handle you at your worst.

Should you feel comfortable doing so, there's no harm in adjusting your profile and telling the world that you're single. But under no circumstances add "… and ready to mingle!" or "Yeah, watch out bois LOL." Remember that the reason this dating option sometimes succeeds where a specific site fails is that you're relaxed and being yourself. Once you've got rid of the obscene party pics, don't go on a de-tagging spree that leaves you with nothing but the five professional headshots you had taken three years ago for the "Meet the team!" section of your employer's website. And don't start writing a load of posts claiming you're off to a super-obscure art exhibition when you're really going down the pub. You're trying to meet your match, not your mum.

However, you might want to minimize the evidence of any exes who are still lurking in your life. If you haven't already defriended and unfollowed them, and you really don't want to, make use of any mute options and filters that will stop them from popping up on your profile, and you from appearing on theirs. Having a former partner filling up your feed is not good dating karma, and if either of you are still tempted to post the odd, "Hey, what's up?" you're going to scare off any potential love interests.

One of the reasons why dating is difficult is that it can be hard to get the balance right. Maximizing your romantic opportunities on social media should be a fairly low-effort project, but it does require some thought. It's always good to be a reasonably savvy self-editor, and if you think any information you share might come back to haunt you, just keep it off the internet altogether. However, the reason these sites and apps are so successful is that they encourage us to curate a broad range of information about ourselves. You're not building a robot – you're painting a positive yet honest portrait of yourself. And chances are that the person you're pursuing online will have a whole sheaf of embarrassingly earnest status updates and terrible drunk photos too. We're all human, and sometimes the best bonding moments happen when you compare flaws.

> *...if you think any information you share might come back to haunt you, just keep it off the internet altogether.*

What to Watch Out For

The most obvious point to make about off-grid online dating is that it can be very hard to tell who is and who isn't single. You might have made it clear immediately, but the biggest upside is also the greatest downside. You're in a virtual environment where not everyone is looking for a hook-up. There's every chance that you'll spark it off with someone who's already attached and being friendly, and in the worst-case scenario you'll spend some time on heavy reciprocal flirting with someone who is already spoken for.

The best way to handle it is to trust your instincts and be perceptive. Treat it as you would a Friday night in a bar with your friends, and look for the cues. If someone is talking a lot about their everyday life online, it will be impossible for them to hide a partner for long.

Safety deserves extra attention when you're outside the confines of a dating site. We've already talked about the precautions you need to take as a matter of course, but you should really lock it down on social media. Because you're surrounded, albeit digitally, by people you already know, love and trust, it's very easy to let your guard down. If you're flirting with someone who can see exactly which postcode you're in when you check into your favourite restaurant, you leave yourself open to potential harassment and unwanted attention. The majority of people you meet online are nice, normal, and unlikely to "just turn up" when you're ordering cocktails, but it's always good to be cautious and avoid leaving a digital trail. Obviously, never check into your own house. That's an idiot's move and no good can come of it.

It's also important to remember that getting to know someone on social media is no substitute for the real deal. You can build up an increasingly vivid picture of someone on screen without even meeting them properly. This can kill the magic and excitement of a new relationship. It's hard to feel joy and anticipation about getting to know someone properly when you've been following their online posts obsessively and could pass an exam on what they ate for lunch every day for the last three weeks and where they've been buying their socks.

It's also easy to let on accidentally how much you've been looking at their stuff, and sound a bit weird. For example, you might go out for dinner and your date will have an anecdote about a hospital visit. Do not say, "Yes! I know! In 2003! I saw all the pictures on Facebook! I liked your mum's hair back then. Does your dad still wear that strange sweatshirt with all the Japanese cartoons?" If the person you're with doesn't think you're a desperate dork, they'll be attempting to take out some kind of injunction that forbids you from ever using the internet again.

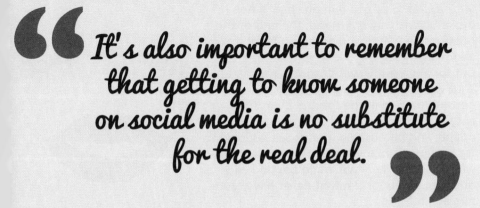

It's also important to remember that getting to know someone on social media is no substitute for the real deal.

"It Happened to Me!"

The following people have all found online love on the road less travelled. They managed to meet the matches of their dreams while busy playing hashtag games, messing about with Farmville and Instagramming sunsets. Here's how it happened.

Caitie, 32, met her fiancé on Facebook

"I met a guy at my cousin's party years ago. We only spoke briefly. He was really good fun but I had a boyfriend at the time and I didn't really think anything of it. But everyone who went to the party was tagged in a few pictures, and we all ended up adding each other as friends. So this guy would pop up on my feed every so often, and he was always really funny. I'd try to make him laugh, adding jokey comments to his funny posts, and after doing this for a few months, it felt natural to talk to him on chat. When I broke up with my boyfriend, the end of the relationship was documented on Facebook, and this guy said he'd love to take me out for a drink if it wasn't too weird. That was three years ago, and we're getting married in the spring. It was so easy to develop a chilled-out friendship online, and because neither of us was looking for romance when we met, the whole thing was pressure-free. If we hadn't added each other on Facebook, I might never have seen him again."

Rebecca, 29, met her boyfriend on Instagram

"My boss asked me to find a photographer for a project we were doing – we didn't have a massive budget, so I used my initiative and looked online for a talented amateur who might be up for doing the work for a more modest fee. I was looking for people working in the local area, and this one set of pictures blew me away. Ironically, they weren't right for us, as we needed a portrait photographer and these were impressive, brooding landscapes. But I sent the guy a message to tell him how much I liked them, and asked if any were available as prints. We met for a coffee, and hit it off. We've been dating for six months."

Lucy, 27, met her boyfriend on Twitter

"Someone retweeted a joke into my timeline, and I started following the guy who wrote the joke. We'd talk on Twitter most days, and we had so much in common that we decided to go for a drink, and that was that! When I've been single before, I've found it difficult to approach men directly, even on a dating site, because it makes me feel quite vulnerable. You're essentially saying, "Um, hi, do you fancy me?" every time. But Twitter moves so fast that you can't take it personally if someone does ignore you, and every interaction is less pressured. Because of that, I find it much easier to be myself, and I'm sure my confidence makes me more attractive."

Even if you're just in it
for the short term, that
doesn't mean you have to
be any less fussy...

CHAPTER 10

· · · · · · · · · · · ·

Keeping It Casual

· · · · · · · · · · ·

Short-Term Romance

Not all romantic endeavours are going to end in Hollywood-style concoctions of chiffon and confetti, and nor would you want them to. Relationship requirements are as varied and individual as the person looking for a partner. You might be hoping to meet someone who will raise a family with you, or at least commit for as long as it takes you to work out the optimum drill speed when constructing a bathroom cabinet. Equally, you might be after something purely physical. If that's the case, you're incredibly well catered for online. But even if you're just in it for the short term, that doesn't mean you have to be any less fussy if you don't want to be.

Casual sex can be super-fun – and super-risky. Most people can pick someone up in a bar and have a lovely time with them on a consensual basis in which no one gets axe-murdered. However, all interactions with strangers have the potential to make you vulnerable, and this is where the internet comes into its own. It's a little easier to run a background check. However, there's no foolproof method of making yourself safe. But you can become safer by using online dating tools to stay extra vigilant and ask all the right questions.

Some people believe that the more casual the anticipated encounter, the less money one spends from the outset. However, if you have spare cash, there is no harm in flinging it at the screening process. It's so easy to find people to sleep with on the internet that it's good to be a little discerning. It's the difference between drinking in a cosy bar with great service and a choice of premium spirits, and hanging out in a pub the size of an aircraft hangar on a strip-lit industrial estate.

Keeping It Casual

If you're into messages with crude spelling and even cruder content, graphic pictures, descriptions and demands, you'll find what you need easily and probably without much help or instruction, but still stick to well-lit areas, find out your date's surname, tell everyone where you are, leave the GPS on your phone and don't get into any vans. However, if you want to be seduced with something approaching subtlety, you'll need to code your words carefully and cleverly. There's plenty of disappointing sex to be had on the internet, but that isn't worth anyone's time or effort. Craft your profile skilfully and you'll start to see what all the fuss is about.

Sadly, there are a few online cads who are all "starlight" this and "honeymoon" that and "when we get a puppy", only to disappear immediately the morning after, if not during the night. Don't be that dude, dude. It's tempting to make someone believe they have a future with you in order to get into their pants, but it's downright unethical. You can be clear yet elegant in spelling out exactly what you want, and how long you want it for, without attracting the wrong element or making your mother blush. Here's how it's done.

Profile Buzzwords

The construction of your casual dating profile is as much about what you leave out as what you put in. If you've ever looked for a serious relationship online, don't be tempted to recycle your old words. You're going to need a whole new approach. You're just looking for someone you fancy. There is no point banging on about your fondness for Bach or describing your inimitable way with risotto.

Think about the specific things you'd like from the relationship. There's no need to be explicit. Is it going to be entirely bed-based or are you hoping for someone to go to the movies with as well? You want to establish that you'll have something to talk about together – just avoid painting a picture that sounds too domestic.

The first words that you'll make use of are probably "short-term", "casual" and "fun". Within reason, you can be as shallow as you wish, as you're not looking to impress anyone with your cerebral qualities. It's tempting to list your ultimate turn-offs and advise anyone who answers to that description to stay the hell away, but be positive. Describe your dream partner in as much dramatic detail as you wish. Think hard about what makes you really, really feel attracted to a date. You might end up meeting someone who is, objectively, one of the hottest people in the world, but struggle to create chemistry with them.

"

Is it important that they have a great taste in fragrance, or a sexy hobby, or a deep laugh?

"

Do you feel more comfortable with talkers or listeners? How much does the sound of someone's voice matter to you? Is it important that they have a great taste in fragrance, or a sexy hobby, or a deep laugh? Remember that when you're planning to get physically intimate with a new person, you'll both need to feel comfortable together quite quickly. If you're confident when it comes to looking online, you're probably great at putting people at their ease and winning them over with your confidence. However, the person you're pulling needs to be as laid-back as you are if it's going to work. Shy guys need not apply, and your profile should make it clear that you're looking for someone fairly forward, otherwise things are going to get awkward.

Pictures are important but they do not have to be gynaecological. Use a good, clear headshot, something full-length and perhaps a fun option for luck. Aim to look happy as well as sexy – if you're super-sultry, suitors may worry that they need to know all sorts of complicated tricks with oils and ropes before they can approach you. However, if that's what you're into, smoulder away. Wearing bright colours will make sure you catch all the right eyes and fast-track you to a speedy, sexy time. Red dresses are erotic clichés for a reason.

Setting the Tone

Because you're looking for a proper, real-life encounter, it's in your best interests to get your crush offline and in a well-lit place as soon as possible. If the person is too vague or more into messaging than meeting, cut them off. This may seem harsh, but online dating is busy and results-driven, and ain't nobody got time for shyness or ditherers.

Unless some combination of hormonal and interplanetary alignment means you just cannot help yourselves, try to make sure the first meeting is sedate and straightforward. Arrange to meet for a coffee or cold lemonade somewhere central, and be frank about your requirements and the fact that you're sizing each other up. If you're definitely in the market for something completely casual, you cannot overstate this enough. There's a chance that the person you're meeting will also be looking for a relationship, and they'll want to know why you aren't. There is no harm in hinting that you may be about to leave the country, start a new job, embark on an intense period of study – any life event that might prevent you from wishing to start a new emotional connection will do. You don't have to lie outright, just keep it vague.

During your first meeting, you'll want to bring the combined observational skills and deducible powers of Belgium's top detectives, Tintin and Poirot. It's scarily easy to be swayed by a pretty face and forget to ask any important questions, in the same way that you might be so charmed by an estate agent's chatter that you'll forget to ask whether the house has a working boiler. There's a chance that anyone responding to your casual call-out will already have someone, or something, complicated waiting for them at home. That is a situation you want to avoid at all costs. Some people might argue that infidelity is the business of the cheater alone, but if you inadvertently collude in something ethically dubious, you might face a range of distressing issues further down the line. The worst-case scenario involves litigation, and the least awful one will probably get you a slot on a new reality show.

If someone is insisting they're single but refers to "our dog" or "when we went to Santorini and our sunburn required medical attention", tread very carefully. Similarly, plenty of people claim to be in open relationships, but when you meet someone for the first time and they claim that their partner is happy for them to play away, don't take it at face value. Request a meeting between the three of you, either face-to-face or via Skype. It might feel a bit weird but it's better to do that and get everything out in the open than risk being cited in someone's divorce.

Although it might be the antithesis of romance, this is a good time to talk scheduling. How much time do you have, and how often would you like to see someone? It's no good having a hook-up who wants to hang out twice a week when you only have an hour a month to spare. When you're dating and looking for a relationship, a little mystery can be a great thing. But when it's all physical, you need to be more blunt and upfront than a talent show judge critiquing a talentless glamour model's rendition of "Like a Virgin".

It's scarily easy to be swayed by a pretty face and forget to ask any important questions...

Breaking It Off

If you stay focused and hopeful, you and your online hook-up will have many happy weeks of swinging from the chandeliers and peeling each other off the ceiling. However, make sure you manage your fun. It's easy to let the situation slide into a relationship if you're not keeping track of it – unscheduled bonus sexy times, meals out and trips to the zoo indicate that things aren't staying as casual as you originally planned.

As long as you're both disciplined at sticking to what you signed up for, this won't be a problem. Also, if you're both happy to hang out more regularly and talk about meeting each other's parents, that's wonderful – some happy endings do lead to the happy ending. However, there's a chance that one of you might become more attached than the other, especially if you are becoming increasingly involved in each other's lives. Let mindfulness be your watchword. OK, it's not an especially sexy word, but you need to make sure your wishes and priorities aren't changing.

In the event that you notice your new friend is getting a bit more into it than you are, you owe it to them to be brutal. Call it off as soon as it gets too cosy, because the longer you leave it, the harder it will get – and the more time you will both have to pursue separately what you really want. If you're the one whose feelings change, you need to alert your sexy-times pal as soon as possible. Tell them you appreciate that it's unprecedented and not what they signed up for. There's a chance that they might feel the same way as you, but don't pin your hopes on it. Sometimes you discover what's truly right for you when you start doing what you want but it stops working. The good thing is that you can go back online and alter your approach in order to look for new possible partners.

Also, don't forget that chemistry fizzles out. If the action stops being fun with your new flame, call a halt to proceedings. Casual sex works when you've got the confidence to go after exactly what you want, and your desires are going to evolve over time. As long as you're clear in all your communications, you've got nothing to lose by saying what you think. Otherwise, it's the sexual equivalent of ordering the same flavour pizza every time, even though you've developed an anchovy allergy, just because you don't want to hurt the delivery person's feelings.

> "...unscheduled sexy times, meals out and trips to the zoo indicate that things aren't staying as casual as you originally planned."

Online examples of true romance are everywhere. We just don't hear the happy stories with the same frequency that we encounter the mad, sad ones, for obvious reasons.

CHAPTER 11

• • • • • • • • • • • • • • •

Happy Endings

• • • • • • • • • • • • • • •

True Love

There's probably someone in your life who hates the internet: an aunt, a colleague or a particularly voluble neighbour, who likes to volunteer their opinions and answer questions that no one has asked. "I don't know why people can't just talk to each other!" they'll whinge. "All day long, tap, tap, tap, everyone with their heads down, failing to take part in normal human interactions. It's no wonder you can't meet anyone who wants to share their life with you. It's no wonder you're all alone. No wonder you'll probably end up being found unconscious in front of *Celebrity WAG Island*, half-eaten by your own cat. In fact, you won't even have a real cat soon. It will all be done on a computer, you'll see." These people complain that we're ruining romance because we're looking for a partner with the same methods we use to shop for groceries. But what could be more romantic than jumping into a growing pool of single people who want to find love as much as you do?

To the uninitiated, the internet is a cold, binary land, populated by faceless coders who want to steal all your money, see pictures of your nipples and demand information about your mother's maiden name. But you know better. The internet is made by the people who use it. And sure, there are pirates, robbers and baddies. There are also cads, commitment-phobes, heartbreakers and people who think the letter "h" is pronounced with itself at the start. It's no different from your local park or pub, just a little bigger. And among all the cold, unfeeling idiots and overly hungry cats, there are genuine romantics. Your love story is no less legitimate when it's spelt out in 1s and 0s.

Happy-Ever-After

When you're exposing yourself to a bigger selection of potential matches, you're much more likely to encounter someone who wants the same things as you. Online examples of true romance are everywhere. We just don't hear the happy stories with the same frequency that we encounter the mad, sad ones, for obvious reasons. It's easy to lose faith in the process before you start, when everyone else seems to be going on a series of awful dates, but you might meet 10 terrors before you find someone you adore. The anecdote ratio is weighted to favour the weirder tales. And we're all so naturally curious about the macabre that we sometimes forget to listen to the straightforward fairy tales. A story that starts, "So, we met and he was wearing a false nose because he didn't want to be recognized by tax inspectors" immediately engages you with its own compelling, if grizzly, narrative. On the other hand, "We had a drink and hit it off straight away," isn't particularly interesting as a sentence. But it is fascinating when it plays out for real.

Here are some gorgeous, actual examples of people who found their happy-ever-after courtesy of a keyboard and a screen. Whether you believe in fate or choose to be in charge of your own destiny, you will find something to inspire you, thanks to the people who discovered each other through a combination of clicking and hoping.

Lauren, 26:

"Technology brought us together – but it almost stopped everything before it started."

"I met Matt on MySingleFriend.com. We'd been messaging for a couple of weeks. I really liked him, but I was new to online dating and I didn't immediately think, 'Oh my God, he must be the one!' I was happy to reserve judgement until we actually saw each other in real life.

Our first date wasn't great. We went to a bar, and I was nervous about telling him that I didn't really like drinking, in case he thought I was weird – I sometimes have an allergic reaction to alcohol. I was so scared I was going to be sick that I was really quiet on the date, and Matt thought that meant I didn't like him! He still sent me a message afterwards saying he'd love to meet up again but would understand if I wasn't into it, so we arranged a daytime date. He was planning to show me around a local market.

We were quite casual about timings, so I started to get worried when I texted him to say I was on my way and didn't hear back. I waited half an hour for him, and then messaged my friend to say I'd been stood up and was heading home. I was about to get an underground train, when I saw a store I loved and thought that I could salvage the day with a little shopping. After another 20 minutes, Matt phoned me, wanting to know what was going on. He hadn't received any of my messages and thought I'd stood him up!

That was four years ago, and now we're living together. If I'd been underground when he phoned, we would have missed each other completely. Thank God for shopping!"

Meg, 32:

"It was supposed to be an internet holiday romance, but now we're engaged"

"When I went to visit a friend in LA, I knew she was going to be working during the day and I had to figure out a way to entertain myself. A few friends had mentioned that they had used Tinder on holiday before, and as long as you were safe and sensible, it was a great way to meet locals. If you met a hot guy, all to the good, but if nothing else, you'd make a new friend who was happy to show you around the area and, in my case, stop me from spending the whole trip sat on my own in a Santa Monica Starbucks.

I met a couple of sweet guys, and it was all quite casual, then I started hanging out with Mark. I knew it could only ever be a holiday fling, but Mark was so much fun and so easy to talk to that I was really sad when I had to head back to London.

I kept telling myself that I had no right to be sad, and I knew what I was getting myself into. But we kept in touch, and I was over the moon when I got a message from him after a few weeks to say his work was sending him to the UK.

We had the best time together in London, and decided to make a go of things long distance. A year later, I've just moved to LA and we're getting married in the spring. Tinder is AWESOME."

Shontelle, 28:

"I was about to cancel my subscription"

"When I met my boyfriend, I had been on so many bad internet dates that I thought the universe was playing a joke on me. There had been Vintage Guy, who wore a monocle at all times, despite having 20/20 vision. Then Surf Dude, who stood me up three times to catch some righteous waves – I mean, he used the word 'righteous' in his text message. And the guy who seemed to get off on correcting my table manners, telling me that I wasn't holding my fork properly. I'd logged on to cancel my subscription when I saw the message from Dan. It was short and jokey, and made a reference to *The Royal Tenenbaums*, which I'd mentioned in my profile as being one of my favourite films. I thought I'd go on one last date and then never look online again.

I kept waiting for Dan to do something insane, but he was lovely. I think I fell for him because everyone else I'd met seemed to be working so hard to cultivate this persona, but he seemed totally happy in himself.

After a couple of years, I've stopped holding my breath, waiting for him to do something insane. He's the love of my life and we've started looking for a place of our own."

Priya, 31:

"My online match wasn't into me, but I fell for his friend"

"Even though I didn't actually meet my boyfriend on Match. com, I hold them responsible for everything! A couple of years ago, I went on a few dates with this guy called Tim. He was really cool, he was into art, he was cute – but he just wasn't quite right for me in a way that I couldn't put my finger on.

He felt exactly the same way I did. We both admitted there was no spark but we wanted to stay in each other's lives and be friends. All my mates thought this was a bit weird, but we kept hanging out.

When I went to a party at Tim's house and met Eric, I found the spark that had been missing. There was no way I would have found him if I hadn't met Tim through online dating, and my story has inspired all my friends. Even if that guy isn't the one, there's a chance he could end up introducing you to the one.

I've tried to set Tim up with my friends, and so far nothing has stuck, although he is quite keen on my mate Emily, so watch this space!"

Monique, 25:

"Online dating reunited me with my junior school crush"

"My story is a little embarrassing – basically, I met Jake when I was eight. His family was based in South Africa and worked all over the world, so he was at my school for a term. We hung out all the time when we were kids, but ended up losing touch.

I couldn't remember his surname, so I don't think I could have found him on Facebook. I guess I've had a soft spot for men with the name Jake ever since, but I didn't immediately recognize him from his adult profile picture on Plenty Of Fish!

We were messaging pretty casually, but it wasn't until we met for beers and he mentioned his childhood that it came out. I think I said, 'This is going to sound completely crazy, but were you at school with me when you were little?' I was worried that he wouldn't remember me, because he'd been in the UK for such a short space of time, but he realized who I was straight away. In fact, he spilled his beer! He said, 'I knew there was something familiar about you, but I thought that it had to be a coincidence!'

I never used to believe in fate, but I think we both sometimes wonder whether we were meant to be."

Fridja, 30:

"He was living three houses away from me"

"Whenever people claim that meeting people in real life is better than meeting them online, I have to tell them how I met my boyfriend.

I was matched up with Curtis on OKCupid, and it was all quite straightforward. We'd both been looking online for a couple of months, we both had some horror stories and near misses, and we were curious about seeing what was out there, rather than being desperate to find love straightaway, so it was all a bit of a slow burn.

The more I learned about him, the more I liked him, and I was starting to have serious feelings for him. Then he took me back to his place for the first time, and I discovered that his house was more or less opposite mine. We'd both been single and looking for ages, and it ended up with the boy and girl next door!

Even so, I would definitely recommend going online, as opposed to waiting to bump into your hot neighbour. Perhaps some celestial force brought us together in a geographical sense, but I needed the internet to make me realize he existed.

The best thing about it is that he moved in with me last summer and he didn't even need to hire a van!"

How Will You Know When You've Met "The One"?

Modern romance might not be accompanied by the same heart-thumping, handkerchief-dropping, lock-of-hair-gifting pieces of proof we're used to in old-fashioned love stories, but there are a few signs and signals to look out for if you want to know whether you're ready to call off the search. It's usually something you feel in your gut, and when you're ready to settle down, you won't need a checklist. But just in case, here are a few pointers that will tell you that you no longer have to entrust your future to internet algorithms and ultra-flattering photos.

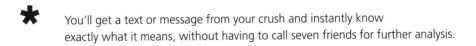

✱ You'll get a text or message from your crush and instantly know exactly what it means, without having to call seven friends for further analysis.

✱ As well as being able to tell them that you sometimes go to the toilet, you'll keep your own box of tampons in their bathroom cabinet.

* They will know all about what you really watch on TV – not just the tasteful Scando box sets listed on your dating profile, but everything the Food Network deems fit to screen, and *RuPaul's Drag Race*.

* You're friends with each other's mums and pets on social media.

* As a couple, you're both such enthusiastic cheerleaders for online dating that you've forced all your single friends to sign up.

* You've had at least one intense late-night argument outside a kebab house or at a taxi rank.

* Occasionally their laundry gets mixed up with yours, and you're both happy to wash each other's socks sometimes.

* You've seen each other's passport photos. And you're still together.

* They know exactly where you stand on kale.

* They've taken you to a family gathering where a drunken uncle has sat you down and told you that, until you came along, everyone was wondering whether your partner was going to end up taking religious orders.

* You're seeing them on Friday nights, Saturdays and bank holidays: primetime dating.

* When your friends ask how it's going, you don't treat them to a confused, three-hour, real-time play-by-play of your last date. You just smile and say, "Excellently!"

* You develop an odd and intense interest in their trivia. You know their preferred brand of deodorant, lunchtime sandwich and air-conditioning setting.

* They trust you with their phone, you've given them your PIN, and you know you can log on to each other's Skype without encountering a semi-naked ex.

* Some of your pals have created a clunky, celebrity-style portmanteau name, just for the two of you.

* You've talked about going public on Facebook. And your status isn't given as "single" any more.

* When you find an especially excellent new YouTube video, you send it to them first.

* They have attended one of your work events and graciously allowed your boss to triumph in the pub quiz.

* You wake up with a smile on your face.

* You have both shut down all your online dating accounts.

True Romance

Fear of freaks and Catfish should not stop you from living your romantic life, but no matter how smart you are, you need to take sane, sensible dating precautions for your own physical and emotional health.

CHAPTER 12

· · · · · · · · · · · · ·

Safety Issues

· · · · · · · · · · · · ·

Taking Care

When you talk to your mum, or perhaps your granny, about internet dating, she will have one question for you, and it won't be: "Is it fun?" or "Where do you go on a blind date?" or even "Have you met the person who will give me grandchildren?" No, it will be: "IS IT SAFE?" To be fair, some mothers are entirely au fait with the online scene and may well have their own **OKCupid** account (and whatever you do, don't look at the profile of hot_mama_69_xox, just in case you encounter something no son or daughter should ever see.) But when online relationships are discussed in the news, they're normally preceded by the words "unprecedented tragedy", "lessons learned" and "found in a suitcase three weeks after the event". So well-meaning relatives who aren't involved in the dating scene may be labouring under the misapprehension that you're paying £9.95 a month to get murdered.

It's natural for family members to worry about whom you're meeting, and equally natural for you to dismiss them as paranoid Luddites, stuck in miserable marriages because they never had the opportunity to fall for someone they had stuff in common with. But your family isn't completely crazy – and they're certainly less crazy than some of the people you could end up dating.

The process of finding a partner on the internet isn't completely danger-free. Arguably, it's safer than it's ever been, as the widening pool of people signing up to dating sites means the risk of encountering a weirdo is diluted – for the sake of argument, it could be one in 100 people and not one in 10. It's easier than ever to run your own mini background check on people with a bit of strategic Googling and a few social network searches. Thanks to TV reality shows like *Catfish*, we know how people might behave if they're about to pretend to be someone, or something, they're not. If they claim to be a Florida-based model and keep having to leave the country because their dog is sick, we know they're about to be shamed on TV and their dog is imaginary.

Still, knowing the risks doesn't make you immune to them, in the way that knowing basic road safety doesn't mean you can waltz into the middle of four-lane traffic singing, "Look at me! I'm dancing with the cars!" without expecting to end the day in hospital. Fear of freaks and Catfish should not stop you living your romantic life, but no matter how smart you are, you need to take sane, sensible dating precautions for your own physical and emotional health. Common sense isn't sexy but a little goes a long way, and it's the only thing that will stop your mother from having to say, "I told you so."

…your family isn't completely crazy – and they're certainly less crazy than some of the people you could end up dating.

Geography Lessons

We all know not to give our addresses to strangers. We're not going to post selfies in which we're grinning and waving our unopened mail for the attention of potential paramours. No one in their right mind would send a flirty message that finishes with a link to their house on Google Earth. You're not going to stand by the street sign at the bottom of your road, holding a notice that says, "Looking for love at No. 23. Come and get it!" But it's alarmingly easy to give away too much information about your location without even realizing it.

Are you in the habit of checking into places on Facebook?

Do you sometimes accidentally tag your tweets because your generous thumbs have slipped on the tiny touchscreen, revealing you're bragging about the glamorous party you're about to attend while standing in the queue at a budget chicken takeaway restaurant?

Do you use the map on your phone, which means that somewhere up in the Cloud there's a record of every date you've ever been on?

We're all a little too relaxed about revealing our location, which means that if someone finds you online and has less-than-honourable intentions, it takes relatively little sleuthing on their part for them to find you.

This sounds very scary, but as long as you're conscious of your behaviour, where you're going and whom you're sharing the information with, you'll be fine. Social networking has made us all very open about who we are and where we are, so when we're meeting people online we have to remind ourselves to hold back. Try not to share too much about your routine, at first. If someone is claiming to go to the exact same coffee shop as you every day, it might not be the adorable coincidence that you want it to be. Look out for specific questions. If someone wants to know which bar you and your friend are going to, or asks for a road-by-road breakdown of exactly where it is that you walk your dog, it's probably not because they're a cartographer looking for exciting places to feature on their latest map.

Some apps and sites, like Tinder, are looking for potential matches for you based on who's in the area. This can be great for instant gratification but it can potentially also expose users to an overwhelming amount of unwanted attention. Most apps take safety super-seriously and would never reveal your exact coordinates to other users. However, make sure you don't blab, "I'm just around the corner!" the second you're matched up with someone – take some time to message them and get to know them a bit first. If you're out and up for some swipe action, bring a friend in a similar situation and you can look out for each other. There's safety in numbers. And never, ever, *ever* approach someone you see across a crowded room with the words, "I recognize you from the internet!" No matter what your intentions are, you'll sound like a stalker.

...make sure you don't blab, 'I'm just around the corner!' the second you're matched up with someone...

Identity Check

Do you remember being warned about stranger danger when you were a kid? Don't wear clothes with your name on because it makes it easy for a weirdo to pretend they know who you are; don't get into cars with people you don't know; and never give the time of day to anyone who asks if you'd like to come and see some puppies. You may be an adult now, but some of the rules are still relevant, especially when it comes to your name.

No one should be able to Google you successfully from the information you disclose in your online dating profile – that means no explicit references to your name, occupation, age or family members. WriterGal222 is fine; LondonTeacherLauren is not. Realistically, it's unlikely that anyone is going to try to track you down before they've spoken to you, but you need to put as many layers and levels of safety between you and your dates as possible, just for your own piece of mind.

Choose a fake name and set up a dedicated online dating email account that you can connect with your profiles. It will help you to keep dating separate from the rest of your life, so you're less likely to give out any compromising information or accidentally forward your company's expense spreadsheet and holiday schedules to your new crush. As an added bonus, when seeing your inbox fill up with messages gets a little too distracting, you can sign out of your dating account while keeping on top of everything else. Well, you probably won't, but you have the option.

> *Although you might not end up on the news, you could find yourself fielding midnight telephone calls from an emotional graphic designer named Garry...*

Lots of people like to talk on the phone before a first date. It's becoming increasingly rare but, occasionally, we like to hear the sound of someone's voice before we commit to sharing a bottle of mid-range rioja with them. You can still do this and stay safe, as long as you're reasonably reserved. Chances are that you always call from a mobile, but if you have a home phone, never give out the number or make calls from it. Chatting  to someone could, and should, make you feel more relaxed and intimate, but if the call goes well, don't start feeling so free and easy that you share details you'd never write in a message, like your life insurance details or a map of where you keep your safety deposit box.

There's nothing to stop you from getting a temporary SIM card and handing out that number. If you end up meeting in real life and starting a proper relationship, you can always tell them you lost your phone. It might sound overly fearful, but it's better to create a bit of extra admin in order not to worry in the long run than it is to throw caution to the wind. Although you might not end up on the news, you could find yourself fielding midnight telephone calls from an emotional graphic designer named Garry, who really, really thought you connected at the silent disco auction.

Buddying Up

We all know how to lay a trail of digital and practical crumbs in order to ensure our friends and family have enough clues, should they need to track us down. We always tell everyone we know whom we're meeting and where we're going, and we promise to text at 20-minute intervals to confirm that we haven't been attacked. In exchange, we have enough messages offering us potential excuses if things are going very, very badly and we need an escape route. ("I think I left my cat… on the oven" makes no sense but, equally, cannot be argued with.)

Within reason, and their own limits when it comes to time and boredom thresholds, it makes sense to involve your close friends and family on every step of your pixel-based path to passion. While you almost certainly know what you're doing and have trustworthy, reliable instincts, you're going to need backup when confronted with the profile of someone who has the face of Hollywood royalty and the written skills of a psychopath. Similarly, good mates will always ask important questions, like, "If they weren't holding that super-cute Pomeranian, would you be bothered by the fact that their face is covered in prison tattoos?"

There's an inverse relationship between what you share and who you're sharing it with. People you meet online don't need to know much about you, but those who love you already should be hearing everything about the new people you're discovering. You might be able to spot a dodgy prospect from the word go, but occasionally you'll have a virtual connection with someone before they start messing you around. Alice's experience shows that if someone has a problem with the way you look after yourself, they're probably not worth pursuing.

Alice, a 28-year-old PR manager, revealed:

"I'd been messaging a guy constantly for three weeks, and even though we'd never met, I had the hugest crush on him. He lived quite far from me, and made a really big deal about coming to my house, picking me up and taking me out for dinner.

"Because I felt like I knew him, I was totally up for it, but a couple of close friends pointed out that it might not be a good idea. The first meeting should always be in a neutral location, whether you've been messaging for hours or months. As soon as I said this to the guy, he got really sulky and weird. I don't know what his agenda was but, thanks to my friends, I realized I didn't have to be part of it. He was selfish and didn't have any respect for my safety. I was disappointed that I never got to meet him, but relieved our relationship didn't go any further when it became clear that he was not a nice guy."

> *The first meeting should always be in a neutral location, whether you've been messaging for hours or months.*

Totes Emosh

So, you've done everything you can to stay safe in the practical, physical sense. But love doesn't come with a risk assessment form. Science has yet to invent a condom for the heart. Your monthly dating fee does not come with insurance – sure, some offer a "meet someone or get your money back" refund, but they won't be able to offer you the appropriate compensation when the love of your life goes off-grid immediately after your fourth date, having suggested names for your children and shown you brochures for a Spanish timeshare they want to buy with you. No site will pay for the frozen pizza you're forced to buy when you get stood up, or cover your dry-cleaning bill when your never-fail date dress, erm, fails.

If you're going to stay sane throughout the process, you need to protect your mental and emotional health with the same circumspect attitude you use to maintain your physical safety. Dating is draining. You're at the mercy of potentially millions of matches, and their issues, insecurities and neuroses, which are going to make the situation feel, at best, a little crowded.

During the dating process, it's vital that you treat yourself kindly, and that you don't take the process too seriously. Geneticists have discovered that anything that stimulates the brain's reward pathways can be bad for you, so a flurry of messages, winks, bumps and nudges might, briefly, make you feel almost high. But if you go through a quiet spell, the comedown and subsequent self-esteem crash might leave you lower than you felt when you got started.

The great thing about being single in the internet age is that you're not alone, and you can always give yourself a boost by bonding over shared war stories. When you open up to your friends, you'll soon realize that everyone has their own personal encyclopedia's worth of bad dates.

Sarah, a stunning accountant in her early thirties, explains:

"I was feeling a bit low one Saturday morning, thinking about how nice it would be to have a boyfriend to cook breakfast with, and I checked my messages. I'd received one from a guy that said, 'You're a 4/10. I'd probably have a go if I was drunk.' It sounds really dramatic but I went back to bed and cried all day. I felt humiliated and completely unlovable. It wasn't until a week later that I mentioned it to my friend, who explained that '4/10 guy' had profiles on most major dating sites and sent that message to all women to get a reaction. I had to laugh – I'd spent a whole weekend moping about a man who's clearly damaged, desperate and determined to take advantage of women with low self-esteem."

Sarah says the experience taught her a valuable lesson. "I have to stay confident and believe I'm worth dating, otherwise the idiots out there will get me down. But my friends help me to have a little perspective, and to remember that if someone's rude at any stage in the dating process, they're probably a bit unbalanced."

> **During the dating process, it's vital that you treat yourself kindly, and that you don't take the process too seriously.**

"...the internet allows us to engage in super-speedy, drive-thru relationships, where you have the opportunity to engage with many people in a seemingly meaningful way."

But what about the perfect partners who make the leap offline, seduce you straight away and then never call you again? It's also usually the behaviour of someone who isn't psychologically healthy. Most relationships aren't perfect, and you're supposed to spend months and years growing to love each other's fabulous flaws. But the internet allows us to engage in super-speedy, drive-thru relationships, where you have the opportunity to engage with many people in a seemingly meaningful way. "Love fraud" is surprisingly common, and you only need to Google "Catfish" to discover that fake relationships are as much a part of the online dating scene as breadsticks are at a buffet. It can be tricky to avoid these situations, as they're usually being masterminded by expert liars, but you can try to keep on top of them with vigilance. Ask as many questions as possible and be suspicious of evasive answers, lost passwords and unlikely sounding medical emergencies. If someone sounds too good to be true, they are. After all, how many billionaire software developers are also fitness instructors, for fun, in their spare time?

Security Checklist

Cut this out, keep it in your wallet and consider getting it laminated, lest it gets covered in soggy, salty tears, rendering it unreadable.

The checklist is the dating equivalent of the fire assembly point map on the back of your hotel room door. You think you'll never need it, until you really need it. Then you'll be sorry.

• •

Security Checklist

☐ Arrange for your first date to be in the busiest, brightest, most bustling place you can think of. Set up a Google alert for flash mobs in the area, and head to those locations.

☐ If your date keeps making allusions to a period of their past that they're "not legally allowed to talk about", it's not going to be a good story involving a lottery win and a Nobel Peace Prize. Make your excuses and stop replying to their messages.

☐ Never Tinder alone. Always get a second pair of eyes on your quarry before you swipe. Otherwise, you don't know who's going to come along claiming they know you "from the internet" before helping themselves to your nachos.

☐ Consider hiring a security guard for your date. You'll look cool and safe, your date will be impressed and you could end up with a backup goodnight kiss if the evening doesn't go quite as you hoped.

☐ If you feel self-conscious about carrying a personal attack alarm, you could wear a giant alarm clock around your neck and tell your date it's a sartorial tribute to Public Enemy rapper Flavor Flav.

☐ Before you leave the house, do an anticipatory Google of your date's name alongside the search term "known arsonists".

☐ Make sure your pepper spray is handy, and keep any safety devices close to you by wearing them under a big hat.

Glossary of Terms
Dating Database
Index and Credits

Glossary of Terms

The internet is no longer a nerds-only space, but some of the old-school geeky jargon still lingers, like a pair of abandoned sweaty socks at the bottom of a gym bag. It's rare that you'll encounter people who don't just say what they mean, but many daters like to throw in the odd speedy acronym to make messaging faster. After all, everyone is into instant gratification, right? You'll be familiar with some of these letters and phrases. Some will make you feel as surprised as your mum was when she found out LOL didn't mean "lots of love".

ASL: Age, sex, location. This is usually a question asked when, for whatever reason, you're on a site where you don't have a completed profile or when the questioner has fallen for many fragrant ladies online, only to discover they're all plumbers and pensioners living in John O'Groats who answer to "Dave".

BDSM: Bondage, discipline and sadomasochism. If you're on a sexy site and you're talking fetishes, this might come up early on, and you'll know exactly what they mean. If you're on a more general site and someone has just suggested it as an alternative to afternoon tea, you might want to do a little research. If it's not for you, you can reply with YKINMK (your kink is not my kink).

Booty call: When the person you've started seeing wants to go on a date. At their house. At 3 a.m. It doesn't usually lead to a story that you want to tell your grandchildren. And when someone booty calls you, you're probably not going to end up with mutual grandchildren.

Catfish: Named after the movie and associated TV show, a Catfish is someone who creates a fake online persona and is not who they say they are. Catfish are rare, but deadly. If someone has a baffling array of reasons for not meeting you, suddenly contracts a rare and fatal illness, or wants you to make friends with their friends on Facebook before you've actually met, be very afraid.

DTF: Down to fuck. If a suitor's first contact with you is a message asking if you're "DTF", you can probably safely assume that they're not planning on meeting your parents or taking you on a romantic trip to Italy.

FWB: Friends with benefits. If the person you're falling for has said they want one of these, you're not going to marry them – they're after an easy-going, commitment-free association based on having a couple of beers and going to bed. At the end of the Justin Timberlake/ Mila Kunis film of the same name, the "friends with benefits" fall in love. Don't hold your breath.

GSOH: A good sense of humour. If a potential date claims to have one of these, don't take their word for it. Insist that they prove it by making you laugh.

Hook-up: A casual, physical fling, which could involve anything from a desktop smooch to a situation in which you're asking the receptionist at a fancy hotel if you left your knickers in the fountain in the foyer.

IRL: In real life. This is online code for "Get off the internet, open the curtains! It's nice outside." If someone wants to meet IRL, romance might be about to blossom. If they have no interest in doing anything IRL, they're clearly a Catfish.

ISO: In search of. For example, "ISO the woman of my dreams." Or "ISO someone with a back garden and a full tool kit who won't ask too many questions."

LTR: Long-term relationship. If they're looking for one, you'll both be on the takeaway Chinese and box sets within the month. If they've just come out of one, they're going to be haunting bars like a thirsty ghost.

NSA: No strings attached. This is even more uncommitted than FWB. Don't misread as NASA and think you've pulled a sexy astronaut.

Sexting: Definitions vary, and sexting may include a messaging someone with a description of a sexual act or a picture of your primary and secondary sex organs. Sexting is allegedly responsible for all the evils in the modern world,

yet it's enormously popular with the twenty-something single set. Proceed with caution – don't send anything incriminating to anyone you don't know, and don't accept sexts you didn't ask for.

Snapchat: A messaging service that allows users to send each other images that disappear after a maximum of 10 seconds. Perfect for sexting.

Swipe left: The action performed on a prospective Tinder date that you don't much like the look of. Repeat users will attempt to swipe left IRL, too. Swipe left is the dating equivalent of pointing at someone and saying, "Boooo! BOOOOOOO!"

VGL: Very good-looking. Usually used as a self-describer by people who won't deign to put up a profile picture.

WhatsApp: A free messaging service with a degree of anonymity. Perfect for messaging internet matches without giving them your actual email address or phone number.

WLTM: Would like to meet. A polite way of saying ISO. It's also not too restrictive: "I'd like to meet women between 18 and 85, with their own hair and teeth, but I'll take anyone!"

YKINMK: Your kink is not my kink (see BDSM.)

The Dating Database

We have here named the top UK, Australian and North American online dating websites, though there are many many more niche sites to be found!

Adults (www.adults.co.uk)
A UK-based site that offers a whole range of options for those looking for love, from city-specific dating to divorced dating, dating for single parents, Christian dating and gay dating.

Badoo (http://badoo.com)
A pressure-free social network for single people looking to pursue friendships as well as relationships.

Dating Direct (www.datingdirect.com)
This site does what it says on the tin, and operates all over Europe – but it does send you bespoke emails listing six specific members you might be interested in.

Dattch (http://dattch.com)
The brainchild of talented tech entrepreneur Robyn Exton, this is a new super-sleek social network for lesbian and bisexual women.

Doing Something (www.doingsomething.co.uk)
A UK city-linked site that matches users based on their preferred cultural activities.

eHarmony (www.eharmony.co.uk; www.eharmony. com; www.eharmony.com.au; www.eharmony.ca)
A subscription site available in a range of countries that specializes in long-term matches based on a comprehensive questionnaire and matching process.

Elite Singles (www.elitesingles.co.uk; www.elitesingles.au; www.elitesingles.ca)
For educated professionals who are serious about finding a partner who works and plays hard.

Gaydar (www.gaydar.net)

A free site and database with personal ads and dating advice for the gay community.

Gaydar Girls (www.gaydargirls.com)

A dating site specifically designed for gay women.

Grouper (www.joingrouper.com)

Grouper is a service available in the US and London that matches your group of three friends with another group, based on Facebook profiles. The people behind the website then pick a bar or venue for you to meet and even throw in a free round of drinks to get your evening started.

Guardian Soulmantes (http://soulmates.theguardian.com)

One of the most popular UK broadsheet-affiliate dating sites. For singles of a left-leaning political persuasion.

Happn (http://www.happn.fr/en/)

Inspired by Tinder, this downloadable app syncs with your Facebook account to link you with matches you've walked past in the street.

JDate (www.jdate.co.uk; www.jdate.com)

The leading Jewish dating site, offering a global social network with plenty of communication opportunities to help Jewish singles find their soul mates.

Lovestruck (www.lovestruck.com/uk; www.lovestruck. com/newyork; www.lovestruck.com/sydney

A subscription site for people searching for love in London, New York and Sydney that finds potential dating matches based on users' locations, interests and the cultural and social activities they enjoy.

Match (http://uk.match.com; http://us.match.com)

One of the busiest dating sites in the world, offering community tips, advice and real-life dating events such as cookery classes and singles nights.

Meet Me (www.meetme.com)

A free social-networking site for the mobile phone generation, created as **myYearbook** by two American high-school students.

Muddy Matches (www.muddymatches.co.uk)

A growing website for people who love the great outdoors.

My Single Friend (www.mysinglefriend.com)

A UK subscription site in which all prospective daters are vetted and rated by their best friends. In theory, this stops anyone from missing out because they can't blow their own trumpet or disappointing their date through exaggeration. However, the profile writer might just want to get their single friend off their hands and into the arms of a third party.

Oasis (www.oasisdating.com)

A free social network for daters with a popular instant-messaging feature.

OK Cupid (www.okcupid.com)

A free site that has been described as "The Google of online dating". Very popular internationally and with students.

Parship (http://uk.parship.com; http://www.parship.com)

A site for people specifically looking for longterm relationships, this links you to prospective matches using a very thorough personality test.

Tastebuds (http://tastebuds.fm)

This site brings people together based on their taste in music.

Plenty of Fish (www.pof.com)

Another of the big international sites, Plenty of Fish is a free dating website that offers "plenty of choice", although not everyone on the site is looking for something serious.

Tinder (www.gotinder.com)

An enormously popular and free dating app, available internationally, Tinder links you up with other local, single users via pictures from your Facebook profile. Its game-style interface means it's loved by non-singles, drunks and gangs of people in pubs.

Uniform Dating (www.uniformdating.com/en-gb; www.uniformdating.com; www.uniformdating.com/en-au; www.uniformdating.com/en-ca

Uniform Dating, a site available in the UK, US, Australia and Canada, specializes in matching people who work in uniform – or who want to date those that do!

Zoosk (www.zoosk.com)

A desktop site with a supplementary app that works using your Facebook account.

Index

Author Acknowledgements

Love and Thanks to Dale Shaw, Diana Beaumont, Lauren Bravo, Angela Clarke,
Lisa Edwards and everyone on the Carlton team and all the people I have ever met
on the internet. Thank you for inspiring me, and not axe-murdering me.

Picture Credits